Motherhood
Minus the Medals

Nelly Bryce

For all the guilty mothers.

When something is beyond all explanation.
When it feels like an impossibility to describe.
That's when poetry steps up to the plate,
bold as brass or quiet as a whisper and replies,
"Let me have a go".

Contents

Prologue by Nelly Bryce

About the Author

Prologue— I Never Wrote It For Them Anyway

I lost myself for a while after becoming a mother. Truth be told, some days I am still finding myself again now, ten years and four children on.

I also unleashed a fury that I have felt in the background of life for a long time, perhaps ever since I was very young, brought up by a strong single mum who taught me that women can do anything, but then entering a world intent on enforcing the opposite.

A fury exasperated by the discrimination I experienced at work after entering parenthood and the accompanying realisation that, if the world needs more women in leadership positions, more women to be fulfilling their potential in every area of life, which it so urgently does, that this will simply not happen until we address how society treats women at this stage of life.

I can't say that I planned to write about this, or the intriguing, interesting, darker parts of motherhood. The dichotomy of emotions, the extremity of experiences, the paradoxes –how all at once women can be completely invisible and achingly visible. I just find myself slightly obsessed with the deeper parts of life, of being a mother, of being a woman, of being a human being.

Many poems are autobiographical and some are not; I enjoyed the liberation of artistic licence, but some stories do not want to be told by me, so there are topics I considered writing about but didn't. This is in no way a book about every experience of motherhood, it is a book about AN experience of motherhood. It could never be an entire experience even if I wanted it to be because the topic of motherhood is too broad, too immense. There should be entire shelving units in libraries dedicated to it because there is so much to say and learn from. There are not. So, my goodness, I hope that it might inspire you to share your story, because we need to hear every single, vastly different experience, especially the ones which are too often left untold.

Towards the end of writing this book my progress stalled. I saw my children reading it one day and wondering what they did wrong, imagining that I'd spent ten years desperate to unlock the restrictions they had placed on my life as opposed to them being the reason that it mattered so much that there were no restrictions at all. I feared that I would appear ungrateful, decide that the next day I'd revisit the book, add some lighter tales about days out at the beach, remove some of my honesty. Or stop writing it altogether. I'd be a better mother. Like I could possibly write anything which would capture a love this deep. Like there is anything that I'd like for this book to do more than dispel this whole concept of a good or better mother so that we can all get on with spreading our wings a little wider.

Writing this book has allowed me to see that it's OK to want to be a mother, or not to want to be a mother, to want to be some days and not others, to want more than motherhood, as well as to want to inhale every single last breath of motherhood, both of these things, just as urgently and truthfully.

So I decided that I had to let this book find its place in the world.
In the hope of discovering that I am not alone.
In the hope of shining a light on how unnecessarily hard motherhood can be in a patriarchal society.
In the hope of giving us all a break.
In the hope of celebrating everything we do.
In the hope of starting a conversation about everything that motherhood can be.

I never wrote it for anyone else anyway.
I wrote it for me, I wrote it for us, I wrote it for you.

Thank you, my friend.

— *Nelly*

One
Arrive, Part I

Welcome to the wilderness of motherhood

It's chaotic here

brutal

terrifying

it's dark

it will require your body and mind to visit places it knows not exist

It's perfect here

gentle

exhilarating

it's golden

it will enable your body and mind to visit places it knows not exist

You cannot escape
You will want to
You will not want to

Try not to close your eyes

Hold on

Let go

This is it.

Feminist Mothers Club

I found my feminist feet after having my first baby
Previously, I'd spent my time jumping patriarchal
puddles
My privilege allowed me to do this, of course
I naively thought it was possible not just for me,
but for all women
If you played the game and concentrated hard
enough, you could avoid getting too wet
(pull your skirt up a bit, have a sense of humour)

That's what I'd been taught
That's what I would prove (always the good girl)

Never mind the energy it took, following such a
treacherous route
And of course I did put a foot wrong every now
and again
staggering home wearing clothes shamefully
sodden
dishonourable nudges with my own arms to steady
myself

More shame

I turned away from the painful truth that others
were already in knee-deep
Hard to look where you might be heading when it
resembles a cliff's edge
Hard not to hope that you will be the one to prove

a different way down

And then I had a baby

And found myself pushing a pram through
swamp-like mud
Not so easy to jump with a baby strapped to your
chest

The patriarchy cuts its teeth on new mothers

Tender, vulnerable, too often alone (three months
grace, max)
Ideal hunting ground
Even the strongest become unsteady after no sleep
I discovered that no life jackets were held back

Everything suddenly far murkier than before
An underworld of sludgy conversations
A grasping of untethered priorities
Wading well and truly against the tide

And so motherhood
Led me to stop pushing, stop jumping and start
asking
With my old identity crushed like ice
With my old career brutally sliced in two
I craved meeting other women with that same
look in their eye
whom I could ask

Is this really what this is supposed to be like?

Motherhood led to me to hunt for a pack
To search out new ground

I finally realised when I became a mother
That women were never meant to do this alone
That we can continue to trudge our way
Towards a table that we don't even want to sit at
anyway
Finding solutions for problems without
addressing the cause
Or design a whole new path

Yes, I found my feminist feet after having my first
baby
Perhaps it was the sound of small steps right
behind me
Already learning how to leap puddles.

Nelly Bryce

At Nine With Neon Nails

We eat cake and celebrate with neon nails and
new roller skates as her friends sing out loud to
songs with words they don't yet understand, lines
rewritten for a nine-year-old mind; kind, funny,
without wearing that cloak of self-consciousness
yet.

She moves her almost too long limbs to the
rhythms in the air, arms entwined, lips licking
sugary frosting from sticky fingers, wiped on crop
tops and denim shorts, secrets whispered, witty
retorts to our antiquated suggestions for songs
they could play.

I watch laughter rich, head thrown backwards,
long wild hair dancing on partially naked
shoulders, volume rising, the smell of once
lit candies filling the air as I stare transfixed,
momentarily swept up in her carelessness.

Then she holds her hands high and pouts as she
shouts the lyrics to a Beyoncé song, and suddenly
I'm slammed into what I've heard said about
teenage girls all along being "hard work" because
they go out and get drunk and find their beautiful
bodies groped by some jerk.

How do I tell her that she's not got long before
dancing this freely might be seen as wrong, loving

her own body picked apart, the clothes she is
wearing seen in a new light, that if she goes out
after dark on her own that I can't promise her that
she'll be alright.

How do I hold on to the delicate hands of my
nine-year-old with the neon nails and explain
she has limited days of being free from a new
and dangerous type of gaze, that she'll have to
get used to living on edge because even Beyoncé
lyrics might not be enough to stop some boys from
being too rough.

How do I shield her from ads on TV telling her
she's too skinny and friends at school sharing tips
on how to make boys drool, to not second guess
what could happen if she wears that dress or
whether to wear heels when she still just wants to
do cartwheels on the grass?

How do I tell her, and don't say I don't, don't say I
don't because I won't have her slowly accept this
is fate, the cards she was dealt, or worse, her own
fault with how she reacts, I won't have her learn to
adapt to survive like this is just a fact?

I will tell her to keep her head high and her body
strong, I will tell her how sorry I am that we have
still got this wrong, I will teach her to be safe
whilst also to fight for the right to be a child and
a girl with a voice, and I'll promise that I will use
mine for all the girls, who *just* want to dance.

Feminism Drowns In The Un-Cried Tears Of Tough Boys

Why did no one comfort my son when he fell?

Of course they did, everyone is helped,

even the ones who you already describe as 'typical'?

If they want help.

Don't we all want help when we arrive in the world?

It wasn't long before he crawled away from your knee, though, before he ran with a stick in his hand away from a pram.

He did not see himself,

because he was not there.

I don't think so. Now I fear it is becoming too late.

But see how they circle him, he is revered and strong

from a distance.

He is popular, you know that.

They cannot show their affection either.

He cannot be hurt too badly, for he does not cry.

I am so full of the pain that he has had to learn to swallow.

You think you have failed him?

I know we are failing them.

But they will be easily successful.

How is it that you define success?

They will be given everything they want without a fight.

The fighting will still happen, inside and out.

You cannot stop them from being who they are.

Go and put your lips to their cheeks and listen harder,

and then we will understand how to hand power to our girls?

Then we will understand how to cradle humanity in both hands.

One Of Each

Ah great, she grins, *one of each.*

Unearned praise is thrown between us for me to
catch,
but my arms remain awkwardly stiff by my side.
Actually, on my stomach.
Blue and pink balloons swim before my eyes,
both colours tied now to the back of my chair.

How grateful I should feel
now my husband will take more of an interest with
a boy.
They'll play cricket together on a weekend
and I can go on a girls' shopping trip, paint our
nails,
perhaps grab coffee and eat sugary, pink cake.

The stench and strength of testosterone
will be cancelled out by hours of mindful
colouring and ballet lessons.
We get to decorate one room with rainbows,
buy sequinned ruby shoes and also jungle animals,
adventurous greens.

The family name will carry on its masculine
descent,
oh, and if I'm lucky, I'll be rewarded with wedding
dress shopping.
One will leave me, but the other will still come

round for tea every week.
Though the first will still be persuaded to swing
by if I can't work the TV.

There will be an easy toddler and a dreadful
teenager.
One will cry and slam doors, and the other will
exhaust me
running around parks.

How grateful I should be–
that I get to do everything,
the fairies and the diggers
and the tea sets and the football.

What a relief that we won't need to try again to get
it right.
That we will have everything,
like we don't already have everything,
like any child, can't be everything.

These are all the things that I am thinking.

And yet,
I am absurdly grateful
to have one of each.

My hand reaching to the edge of my too-
comfortable chair
to unhook the strings, I helped to tie

and let the balloons float away.

Be Everything They Say You Can't Be

I want to burn the candle at both ends
I want to be fierce and gentle
I want to be fast and then really slow
I want to share when I'm happy
and share when I'm sad
I want to be public and private
I want to be everything and nothing I thought I was
I want to be OK getting it wrong
and OK getting it right
I want to be a million different shades
of wrong and right
I want to be first in my jammies
and last up dancing all night
I want to be that girl and now this girl
I want to be one type of mother
and then another type of mother
I want to be here and now and more than a year away
I want to dislike social media and use social media
I want to do that job and then this job and then no job
I want to be on top of my game and still ask for help
I want to be all paradoxes and inconsistencies
I want to not care too much about either
I want to be everything that they say that I can't
I want to be all of that and more
I want to be
I want to be
I want to be.

Go Fuck Yourself

I didn't fuck myself until I was in my late teens.
Which is a fucking travesty. A feminist one. I got
there in the end.
Finally, stuck two fingers up to the patriarchy.

The thing is the boys were at it young, at our
school anyway. Tossing off this, wanking that,
coming all over the chat. I didn't once hear my
mates agree, laugh about how they also had an
orgasm last night. Or three. Was everyone at it in
their beds, or were others batting filthy thoughts
away from their heads? From sex ed, I only recall
a giant speculum. It was supposed to encourage
us to go to smear tests, I think. I don't remember
them saying to sort yourself out. Were the boys
told or no need, inbuilt entitlement let them put it
about.

Perhaps you might argue, boys biology's right
there, right in their lap, but I'm not having that,
there's no way to explain why again and again,
female anatomy doesn't get the right name, why
female pleasure can't have its own home on a
map. Personally I was unsure whether it was for
me, was it really bad to be wanking to that cute
teacher that we had for double biology and what if
I started, and I couldn't stop. Which is, of course,
what happened. At about 19 in a pub one night
some friends met up and, as was always habit, the

girls broke off to more interesting chat and by the end I was off to get myself a purple rabbit. Turns out I'd lost years of decent self fuckery.

I've got young girls now, and it won't be long before I'm teaching them that touching their own body isn't wrong; that their body is their own and sex starts on their own, because what does it say about who sex is for if you can't teach them to understand what they like and how to ask for that more. I hope the next generation are all over the toys and that parents chat masturbation to their girls as well as their boys because there's already too much that men try to control and this is surely one way we can all

stick two fingers up to the patriarchy.

In Response To My Daughter Asking Why I Shave My Legs

Because I choose to.

This is what I have to say.

I like the feel of a blade sharp against my skin,
the time it takes in the shower each day,
the cost of the pleasure.

I'll even pay extra for pretty pink
to match the paper thin cuts around my knees
where my bones have tried to object and now
bleed
swiftly into the water,
which rinses the inkling clean away
down the sink
clean, as clean as can be.

Which means that you can choose too.

This is what I will say.

Huddle your girlfriends together,
gather them close
as close as the blade
as it glides not just up your legs.

Stroke the soft hair covering your beautiful bodies,
coarse, dark, light, however it may be
stare at it straight in the face
and all agree
to fuck that shit.

Two

Arrive, Part II

Which story shall I tell?
The one which makes my family proud,
or the one which makes my friends swoon?
The one which attracts my *ideal reader*,
or the one which grabs the attention of the room?

Tell the story that only you know,
the one which you can tell off by heart;
the version that you don't always show.
That, to me, seems like a good place to start.

Into The Wild

The cottage was warm and habitable
and I was glad for that

The latch slipped into the bolt to secure the door
as if it had been waiting its whole life for the
opportunity
to show what it was made of

I didn't think twice either way, I don't suppose

The table pre-set with everything I could want or
need
and suddenly I knew both
perhaps for the first time
and so I began

Regularly I ate and hourly I grew
my ankles hoarded water like they expected a
drought
my waist became all generous and giving
a swollen peach beyond my knees

My belly button like an island
a beacon guiding cargo to the central depths

Visitors came and left
we swam and drank together
but this was a solitary voyage

and afterwards I would sit and stare out of the
window into the wild
catch the changing colours of the heather with
something like intrigue
trace the tiny marks creeping up the sides of all
that we had planted
before pacing the rooms watching for signs that
anything was out of place
waiting and watching
polishing the metal so hard that it sang
gathering whispers of stories and storing them in
the larder for later
for when I imagined I might stomach them
all the time holding two beating hearts in my palm

And then came the night
when the water burst from its banks
and rushed out, soaking my fair isle socks
flooding every floor so that I had no choice but to
leave
with the used cups still sat in the sink

and the pages I had underlined stacked neatly by
my bed
I planned to return, but couldn't be sure
and so I grabbed what I could
wrapped myself in blankets and began my ascent
The wind brought with it a saltiness from the
waves
which I would taste later upon skin

the path wasn't the one I had expected

nor the one I'd been promised
mud left me scrambling to keep my balance
and cursing the Gods
but my thighs were still strong
and gradually the roughness of the stones began to
give
I had been gifted the light of a full moon
there are those who will tell you that this was a
gift indeed
to see the clouds circling my destination
the place I had dreamt of so many nights

Up and up I travelled
my arms now cradling my belly to stay upright
a groan expelled with every out breath
the drag of the earth beneath my feet
a swift glance behind confirmed what I already
knew
It was far too late

The smell of the once familiar undergrowth
was now pungent like sweat making me wretch
as thunder began overhead
closing in on the base of my spine
twisting my body in two as if I might snap
like the gnarled trunk of a fallen tree
losing myself a little more with each sodden step

Then just as felt I could travel no further
the end moved into sight
the mountain top with the cradle made of clouds

I stumbled

felt the blanket from my shoulders slip
and my body suddenly ripping apart
flesh mixing with gravel
the dirt pushing itself beneath my fingernails as I
plunged into pain
I heard from beyond myself a moan of defeat
the wildness had challenged me
its ways mightier than I ever could have known

the sharpest stab of lightening
showing me all that I would now lose
and with that understanding, it came

A howl guttural and streaked with red
a voice that was mine once before
with soil stuck to my forehead

I deafened the sky
the buttons on my shirt snagging on my hair
as I crawled on my hands and knees
naked now
to where I knew I needed to be
a trail of soundless, inconvenient rage and
heartbreak
–years long
the route behind me
and then for one single split second
there was nothing else–

the stars looked away
the wolf pack delayed their cry
the photograph, if taken
would have been returned blank

you showed yourself to me
and you were everything
and I was everything–

before the wind let out its breath
and I collapsed back to the floor
lying amongst the ferns
that now held out their arms
as I licked my tongue across the skin
of new beginnings

And in homes across the land
fellow wildings would feel goose bumps
at the birth
of one more.

If They Can't Tell You That It Will Be Wonderful

Because it's hard to explain to someone who hasn't seen the sea how just sitting and watching the waves will make you feel more alive, more at home, than you have felt since you yourself were rocked to sleep by the tide.

If they can't tell you that, *it will break your heart.*

Because it's hard to explain to someone who hasn't had their heart broken this way, who doesn't realise that the task cannot be to put it back together so that it beats exactly the same as before, but to learn to open it up to be broken once more.

Perhaps best, then, to tell you nothing at all.

No Place To Be

When I called you from that bench
which was anywhere except for the four walls of
our own house
and you answered your phone mid-sentence
and all I could hear was the unearthly demand of
photocopiers
and distant voices answering phones
and I learnt that it must be time for lunch, and the
chicken wrap smelt so good and
someone asked if you wanted anything picking up
and you said that you were good, thanks
and then asked me

And when I tried to tell you
rain dripping off my hood and down my nose
and heard the sound of your voice drop
the swinging of a door
as you asked me question after question
trying to understand why your wife
who had everything
would be walking the streets this way
sat somewhere neither of us had heard of before,
crying over
nothing

I felt so much further away that day
than 40 minutes (out of rush hour) in the car down
the M62 motorway

So much further away
than 20 minutes up the road to the local church
for the baby group – where everyone seemed to
know where to sit

So much further away
than the 15 minutes I wanted to spend screaming
in the face of the owner of the polished car that
would park right across the pavement, most of the
days I would push a pram into an empty park with
paths no-one seemed to notice were too gravely to
negotiate with a pram

And I want you to know
If you recognise this bench
and how it doesn't matter that it's dirty and damp
because you don't notice, nor smile for longer than
is necessary at the lady with the perfectly pleasant
dog who tells you that it is a nice day for a walk,
and probably don't stay for that long after that
anyway in case someone notices and thinks you're
not happy with what you've got

I want you to know
that you will never be that far away
from me.

Motherhood Hurts

They don't tell you
That it will hurt
That your back will ache
and the bones
in your pelvis will grind

That you'll bleed
That forever your body will be in recovery
That on dark days you'll grieve for the life
you left behind

That you'll miss your old self
Lose track of sentences
and relationships and entire years

That you'll ache
A deep ache
That you will carry around
like an extra limb
As you watch and watch
and watch to check that they don't die
Every second on high alert

That you will cry
Again and again you will cry
That you'll hold on so tight
That your jaw
will permanently stiffen

That you'll hold your breath
That you'll let it go
And it will hurt just as much
Maybe more

That none of your expectations will be right

That you'll break a little
That you'll mend a little
That you'll feel so much more
That this is the deal
that you will gladly take

That you will take
That you will take
That you will take.

The 2 A.M. Army

I think of me in here
alone with my wildness
eyes stinging, arms heavy
nothing left to give,
only my mind to lose

I think of you out there
hearing the same birdsong
signs that dawn is near
and we've made it through another night

I think of us all everywhere
The 2 A.M. army
fighting for every second of sleep
gathering it up frantically as we feed
and rock and deliver our souls
to the cause

I think of this as the darkness shifts
of you in a stained top
of me in an unwashed bed
and I feel my shoulders begin to drop

A Tiny Glimpse of Perfection

When you rub your eyes,
corkscrewing tiny fistfuls of tiredness,
like you're trying to turn off the day.
I always think,
please don't ever stop being this way,
those sticky cheeks that crash into my chest and,
those creases in your wrists that I could dive into.

I always think,
what a perfect movement.
What a perfect example of a life.

That Friend— Who Makes a Mother

That friend
the sunshiny one
who sends something when
she doesn't need to
because her heart is made that way

who is in awe of your
not-yet achievements
who celebrates the parts of yourself
that you are busy trying to hide

who feels like a winning lottery ticket
that you don't recall ever buying
but has left you so much richer inside

who you meet feeling short on ideas
and leave feeling drunk on dreams

who is the pages with the corners turned
in your favourite book
who is the time the train you thought you'd missed
was running late

who is the snowdrop
that will always survive a late frost
who is the one who sends a message
at just the right time

for you to read
and breathe
before securing your wings.

Last Orders at the Milk Bar

I notice tonight
as your little hand plays with my hair
twirls the strands between your fingers
unaware that this is the last time I'll hold you this
way
the last time you'll find me in the dark so easily
like we were meant to stay
like we've been from that first day

We won't speak of this again
I know that now–
I'd like to remind you about how
we spend these nights and days
and how I fed you again and again
in so many ways

But you won't want to hear, it won't belong
in stories we tell, in photos we share
I can try and save this feeling, gather it up but
the moment has already gone

And I feel it deeply, more than your touch
so deep within my heart,
in the bottom of my stomach
the tears now start
I know it must come to an end
but I'm not quite ready to let go

My body will return and life will carry on

and you will forget but I notice–
I notice everything tonight–
the last time we feed in this way.

Expectations

It's OK to hate days like these.
It's OK to feel like the weeks you've been told to
love
are nothing but never ending.

It's OK to want to run away.
It's OK that your dreams are never larger than a
full day in bed.

It's OK to want and need more.
It is OK.

It doesn't mean that you don't love enough.
It doesn't mean that you are not grateful enough.
It doesn't mean that you are going to mess anyone
or anything up.

Come, lie yourself down in the grass this
summer's evening,
stay long enough for the earth to settle beneath
your bones.

Three

Nurture

Do you remember when we used to be wild?
she asks
All those late nights?
Yeah, I say,
running my finger around the rim of my glass.

I look over at my friend who I have seen raise the
future
All those long nights.
We're still pretty wild, I say
Yeah, she agrees, and her smile is thrillingly full.

Butterfly

It is early morning,
and we are on our way to nursery.

She has stopped, *again.*
I fear we will be late
but am momentarily intrigued
by the sight of impulsive flight;
a butterfly landing and taking off at will.
Fragile as tissue paper dappled in dew,
sticky feet landing just long enough
before swiftly moving onwards.

The limits on life, the shortness of days
   I think butterflies only survive for a few weeks
though suddenly I'm unsure of either.
The show stopping colours and unobtainable
symmetry
of which I now notice neither
as I hurry my daughter along

but still this shape-shifting goddess flies.
She dances, with blossom decorating her heels
tiny wings like cymbals
my child, she sings the sweetest freedoms
music only for the ears of the wind
and the wise.

The body of her book flutters open
and shut before my eyes,

truths visible before they're not.
Oh, to be gifted a glimpse
of life
transformed into living.

On Becoming Patient

I am not a patient person. Or rather, I wasn't.

Productivity was my virtue.
Impatience spurred me on–
holidays, parties, new jobs, having babies
with only the smallest age gap in between.

I would always be looking for the next thing,
the next adventure or opportunity.

But a toddler leaves no house without it taking
twenty minutes.
Try as you might to walk straight down a road, you
cannot do this with a toddler without adding in
another thirty. Manipulation and biscuits will help
with speed, as will some sort of wheeled object
and learning to leave everything and everyone that
bit more dirty.

Having children will force you to slow down for
minutes, days and years.
A toddler wastes no energy thinking about
tomorrow. A toddler might not know where they
are going most of the time, but be damn sure they
are going to colour out of the lines of every single
wobbly step of the way.

Curiosity and fascination and joy (theirs) may
well be accosted by deadlines and schedules

and demands (yours) down the darkest and most
dangerous of alleyways but still they will meander
with their arms wide open, with their feet firmly
planted on the floor they will shout: "Look at that
door over there, can we knock and see what's
behind?"

I've learnt to see that a snail which needs moving
carefully off the pavement really is a life or death
situation.

That the clouds which appear to suddenly
resemble a dolphin genuinely won't ever appear in
that exact same way again.

That failing to stop and listen, and understand,
matters of the heart, will almost certainly lead to
the need for even greater patience down the line.

You can try and fight it, and you may well win, or
you can give in, and stop to see what has flowered
in their imagination.

Children know that magic doesn't like to be
rushed, in fact it just won't be rushed, they know
this, and so they experience magic far more than
anyone else.

Magic relies on trust,
trust that there is enough to go around,
trust that good things are in store,
trust that the sun will still rise,

trust that it will be worth the risk,
trust that you will take the steps necessary,
trust in the fact that you will get up patiently
again the next morning and stretch up your arms
to feel for the side of the couch which will help
you pull yourself up to standing, or say yes to the
opportunity that feels way out of your depth,
because what happens next, even when you don't
know what happens next,
will be worth discovering.

Writing this book, too, has taught me about
patience. From lockdowns to full family isolations,
to periods where I just didn't have anything left at
the end of a night to pick up a pen, to work that
needed to be done because it paid me, to periods
when my calm left me. I've learnt to be more
gentle with myself and my daily existence, to value
the process more highly than the outcome, and to
keep going.

The book I have ended up with is one hundred
times better than the one I started with a few
years ago. Don't get me wrong, I did and do have
a consistent writing practise which keeps me
moving forward, one that has had to adapt to work
around so many children and circumstances. I am
all about showing up, but I'm more comfortable
now with the fact that sometimes success is found
in unusual places. Places where we are not always
brought up to look and where children can teach
you to dwell.

Patience isn't always about standing still. It is being patient with how fast you are going. You can be going really fast and still be patient in your process, and vice versa. And I am OK with that. I'm OK with stopping to look up, there is so much to see along the way.

I've learnt how to be patient because I've seen how these times with our children and with our friends and family, are not even ours to borrow. What fools we are, living today, as if we are owed a tomorrow.

Most of life happens when and where we're not looking – in the local park on a rainy midweek morning, during the two-hour chat you have with a friend on the phone laughing so hard that tea comes out of your nose.

I've learnt to rest amidst the dichotomy of feelings which leave me craving for the end of the school summer holidays and wishing that time would just slow the hell down. I've learnt to be patient because this life-long rollercoaster which we find ourselves on, is entirely the point and no-one gets to ride it twice; the end is just that.

I've learnt that patience and procrastination are not the same thing, nor are patience and a lack of commitment to taking action. Both the latter are avoidance techniques whereas the former, is the exact opposite of avoidance. It is being willing to discover the right result rather than racing blindly towards the wrong one, it is trusting enough to stay true to yourself.

Yes, motherhood has taught me the value of patience.
Has taught me the necessity of patience.
Has taught me the joy of patience.

There are plenty of parts of motherhood that I will happily wish away. But when the mundanity of motherhood threatens to swallow me whole, when I am sat on the floor doing the same jigsaw puzzle that I have done 1000 times before, and I am desperate to scroll through Instagram and deepen my suffocation by seeing what other women are apparently doing with their time, when I want that next project finished immediately but have so much on at the weekend that it feels impossible to scramble an hour together that is mine, I take a deep breath (or pick up a pen) and try to find a way to own the moment by remembering that I have in my possession, not a second.
By remembering that, only I, get to decide.

Things I Have Zero Patience For

Blocking the door with, "what's the password?"

Just get the fuck out of my way.

Teaching to tie shoe laces.

Basically impossible, it's Velcro until you can figure it out yourself.

Playing eye spy.

Kill me now, we passed those cows at least thirty minutes ago.

Batting a ball with a kid who can't hit it.

You've got about three attempts mate, and then I'm done, soz.

Apart from that, I'm a very patient parent.

Little Bird

I watch you swoop

You are never still
hopping from grass to chair to step
two footed leaps
further, with every day that passes

Then tonight you stop
slow and hot
so hot that I can see the glow beneath your skin
feel the soft hair damp around your head

And suddenly I must have you close
panic taking a seat in my throat
I must listen in
to your tiny fluttering heart
breathe my breath against your broken wings
hold you in both my hands all night
my baby bird
back now in my nest
fragile as that first day
peering over an edge, I choose not to see
so scared am I of heights

and I see exactly how far it is to fall
wonder why I've allowed myself to climb this high
knowing of course
that only those who climb this high
get the chance to fly

And so I cling to your tiny body
and wait
for the sun to rise
and you to leap out of my arms
once more.

Many Mothers / Over My Shoulder

The shadow of you
is what startles me on this journey

your ever presence
safe and stifling
infecting my words
or trying to

and the surprising thing is
it never goes

Nelly Bryce

Parenting Time

Give me ten,
just hang on.
Won't it wait?

Give me five,
just having—
Won't be late.

Give me two,
Just doing—
Won't be long.

Give me a sec,
just a sec—
Won't be a sec.

OK, fine what do you want?

No, it's still not snack time.

Guilty Mothers Club

I fall in love.

Drinking tins on benches, coffee from cups with
awkward rims in parks, walks, around tables,
across tables, over a round of cocktails (here's
hoping), a round of tears (how are you coping?), a
round of beers, a round of book chat, of silence, of
sweating, of too much swearing, of not getting—

I fall in love.

Dissecting bosses, promotions, demotions, new
websites, new businesses, maternity leave policies
that are far too shite, kids clubs, politics, sex, no
sex, the names of flowers, of animals, hair colour,
maternity pants, the constant waiting for hours
and hours, more sex, no sex, TV shows—

I fall in love.

Passing advice, passing down clothes, carrying
secrets, arranging meet ups, not minding asking
twice, awkward questions, always answers,
celebrating birthdays, our own mini and not so
mini chancers, potty training, forever out when it's
raining, celebrating babies, holding when things
go wrong, giving out crackers, entertaining what
feels like all night long—

I fall in love.

Sharing bodies, discussing vaginas, feeling guilty,
trying to put it behind us, weeing with laughter,
Whatsapping disasters, the stuff you just can't say,
in any other way, to anyone else who would tell
you that it's OK and—

I fall in love with you, my friends.
Every. Single. Day.

A Poem That Has Nothing To Do With My Views On Sleep Training

You could tell it was new from the cry—
desperately high-pitched,
lungs bursting with need,
slicing through the hazy warmth of the garden,
pausing only for bigger-than-itself gulps of hot
breath.

The birds seem to sense the alarm,
quieten for the screams,
my chest begins to burn,
I am also bursting,
pick it up pick it up pick it up.

Alert now, I scan the surrounding houses
but even a light breeze can carry a cry.
It stops—
and then it starts again,
louder and more piercing.
I have read the same sentence on my page twice,
so put down my book
and go there.

Sleep training, she'll tell me;
he's learning to be alone,
like I need to be reminded of what that feels like,
doesn't know day from night.

Her eyes search the room for something she can't
find,
and I can see from her shoulders
that he is not the only one struggling to survive,
tip toeing across newly cracked eggshell,
the blackout blind failing to darken
the perfect picture book on the side.

No, no, no I long to cry,
to grip her tired arms and mother her.
Let me hold him for you.
Let me smell the stale milk on yesterday's clothes.
Let me rock you both to sleep.
I've learnt some new lullabies which I want to
try—
and she gifts me nothing but the softest sigh
compassion, I realise later (yes, I am grateful).

And my heart breaks all over again.
We've spoken too many times before—
I shouldn't have tracked her down like this,
asked her to carry yet more.
And so I move my mind back away,
leave her in peace,
because I know that with a love this deep,
it's possible to suffocate with the windows open.

A neighbour has started to mow their lawn,
as the birds sing diligently their daily prayers
and I return to my book,
remembering to turn the pages
a little bit more gently.

Never Alone / Never More Alone

The swiftness of her smile says, *'you're not one of us,'* but it's too late, my mat is already next to hers on the floor. I curse myself for hearing the ease with which they chat, for noticing their matching wooden teething toys as we massage podgy arms and stretch out these *special moments.* I try to convince myself I've got everything I need at my fingertips.

Later, as we go to leave, the last one will turn at the door, ask if I want to join them.
I'll taste the bitter-sweetness of being an afterthought.
Thanks, I'll say, but I have plans this afternoon and then treat myself to a new, longer route home.

To Read

He holds the pages as wide as his arms can reach.
So wide, the paper threatens to buckle under his
desire.

"It goes like this," he declares.
It goes like this...

And it doesn't, I think.
But who am I to say?

"Listen as I tell you how life is,"
(my usual claim)
I am waiting for the book back.

But see how he has turned three pages at once,
his fingers tracking new lines.

The Battle at Midnight

We've got a waker. My eyes flick open on high alert and a groan leaves my mouth, a bit like an old drunk who doesn't care which particular drink is on offer, but I'm gonna hold my nerve because I'm pretty certain I got up last time so if I lie really still there's a chance I could remain perpendicular. Arms stuck to my sides, it's all or nothing now on red, I'm feeling confident, done this before, the Mexican sleep-off is in force and I see the door, and he's turning over and there's only gonna be one winner and one loser and –

It appears he was adjusting his sleeping position to fluff up the feathers around his totally oblivious head. Bastard. Unbelievable. Damn it, I crawl out of bed. Make as much noise as possible getting out his way, hope for a last gasp, "You stay, it's my turn" as I make my way out the room.

Nothing.

So I spend some time in the dark working my muscles, wonder why my bingo wings persist. I mean, that feels unfair, make a list of things I need to buy this week. Reassure and rock and whisper some more, pace the floor, all the time torn between the smell of a baby's head and oh my god the joy of getting back into bed that is so close I can almost taste it. Oh my bed, my long-

lost friend, with its snugly, soft deliciousness,
though to be fair I'd actually sleep on the floor
right now given the chance, I'd lie down right here
and shiver in my pants and I really wish I'd put a
jumper on coz it's actually quite cold. But I'm on
a roll, final stretch testing the limits of endurance
but now, heavy limbs, mind springs back to life
preparing for the eliminator.

This is it.

My big moment, hours of training and grind.
Get it right, and I'm gonna be experiencing post
get up power, I'll have hit the big time, but one
wrong move, and we all know I'm back for another
hour. Jesus the pressure. What's the right angle?
Could go for a left-hand side drop, but there's a
large precarious looking Peppa Pig on that end,
better to wrangle with the smaller, random George
wedged round the bend.

Here it goes. The drop. Don't rush it, we've come
this far, gentle with the arm then quick like a cat
out the room and into the throes of duvet passion.
OH MY GOD, MY ARM IS FREE. Don't get too
cocky, don't get cocky, tip toe, tip toe tip fucking
toe oh yes I'm heading back to bed this is what I
live for this is what true happiness actually feels
like, I am freeeeee, I am heading home baby, and I
slide my limbs under the covers I hear whispered
just softly,

"*Do you want me to get up?*"

Are you fucking kidding me?

A Small, But Not Insignificant Fact

"Do you know," she asks me
"Sea otters hug when they go to sleep,
so they don't lose each other"
"I love that," I say
"There's poetry in that somewhere."
"Can we do it?" she asks
"Yeah, we can do it," I say

The hum of the playground fades as we continue
our walk home—
her hand slipping tightly into mine.

This Type of Love

"You'll never know how much I love you," I
whisper, as I return the book
and give you a good night kiss.

Because it's more than the cosiness of a just-
tumble-dried towel.
Or the smell of your crumpled up body as I
tuck you up for the second time—
than running my fingertips across the ears of a
particularly soft dog,
or a single salty crisp from a packet that isn't
mine,
more than every shade of colour in a sharpened
pack of crayons,
or when someone surprises me with a huge
mug of tea just as I'd been thinking
that I'd really like a huge mug of tea.

It's more than dancing full pelt around the
kitchen like I'm 12 years old again,
than the moment when someone shouts that
they can see the sea,
more than the peachiness of evening sunshine
behind closed eyes,
than the smell of home-made sponge cake still
in the oven,
than when I have remembered to water the
plants, and they actually stay alive.

"You'll never know how much I love you," I think,
as I leave the door open just an inch,
because it is so much more than this.

First Day

And there it is—
The minutes into days into weeks into months
into years
Your eyes search mine
Have I done enough?
Is the answer ever yes?
I can still feel your body warm against my chest
Smell so sweet
Now I feel your hand in mine, the fingers coiled
tightly, still small, too soon
And you will go
Will you look back?
I long for you to look back, but pray that you don't
Because you will see me broken my little one
And just like that—
There it is.

Last Day And All He Wants Is Ice Cream

Ice cream. This is what he answers
when I ask how him is feeling about this
his last day.

He asks me about ice cream.

And I wonder how he can think about his
stomach—
when in the depths of mine spin thousands of
packed bags and hundreds of hurries out the door.
The glance that meant please don't go, the churn
of that very first day full of fears. How can he eat
when I still feel all the butterflies of first tries and
can't quite swallow how many times I've now not
held his hand, the conversations I've not heard
over these years?

Then he finds my arm— it is lost,
this boy, who has suddenly grown an inch before
my eyes.

"It will be great, won't it, to get ice cream?"

"Yes," I agree,
allowing myself to be shown the way.
"Yes, it will be perfect."

Fearless Wild Child

Here's to you, my fearless wild child
simmering with the brightest light.
Let no one try to tame you—
even those who tuck you up at night.

Your heart, it is so gentle,
your soul outsparkles the stars,
unaware of your fierceness and beauty;
your voice, it travels so far.

Keep on dancing over the rule book.
Keep on asking why,
don't conform
when you want to make miracles or moon dust,
or if you believe the page should be torn.

May you question the stories that haunt you.
May you write your own good on the page.
You're not broken, let no-one try to fix you,
or dampen your perfect rage.

For when others fall into the universe,
slip in just the right place, the right palette,
my wild one, you go paint the sky.

Turn their heads as you spin a new planet.

Nelly Bryce

All the Things Which We Collect

Thinking about the lasts.
Well I know it will make me cry,
but to pretend that they don't hurt,
to deny that they are happening,
doesn't stop the time from travelling,
it just means that I might miss
(and please god don't let me miss)
the chance to say goodbye.
So I'll stay with them,
package up the tiny pieces of my heart,
and when I fear that they will crush me,
when I can't bare to hold them in my hands,
I'll keep them in my pockets or place them gently
on the ground,
knowing that if I wait long enough,
if I can withstand this hour,
that from every single last,
from the bones of these moments
rubbed to dust between my fingers,
a beautiful first will push through.
Which I might just get to see in flower.

Four

Navigate

Motherhood—

like stepping onto an ice rink wearing heels and
a low cut summer dress, holding a couple of gin
cocktails I planned to drink on the other side.

I wish I'd been more prepared.

I'm unsure if you can ever be fully prepared.

I've learnt since that the only solution is to get
comfortable learning to skate, constantly learning
to skate, particularly because the ice is badly
maintained by those in positions of power who
should know and do better.

But learning to skate is easier if you're holding on
to someone's hand.

And there are a lot of us on this rink.

The Return

I'm on my way back.
I don't know how,
as I am still hanging the tiny white vests along a
drying rack.
The days— the coffees, the plays, the sofas, the
days— minute as waiting for each hour in each 24
hours to unfurl
have somehow swept themselves up into one vast
billowing sheet beyond my grasp,
under which we have kicked our feet into the air,
felt the freedom of floating like freshly laundered
fabric,
hair falling across our faces with no-where in the
world to be.
Except now there is
the curiously enticing sight
of neatly folded washing waiting for me
to re-organise the drawers
and go back—
to a before, that doesn't exist any more.
A wardrobe that has been closed so long, I doubt
what's left within.

And you cannot help me here
because you too are nervously feeling your way,
and it's not mine,
which I try desperately to deny
because we were one, just you and I,
but I know that with a day ahead so full of tears

there's every chance we both might drown
if I don't keep my eyes fixed firmly down
upon remaining upright in these shoes
that don't seem to quite fit right (yet),
and somehow find a way back—
To an old which is now a new.

Please see how I have been spun around.
How I have been turned so perfectly inside out,
and am exactly the same and exactly different at
the same time.

Ask me to show you photos.
Let me sit myself down and arrive.
Tell me that I'm doing great, and I will do my best
to hear,
and not hide the snags in my tights,
that give away the year of which I have survived.

But just don't expect me to explain where I've
been,
why my clothes now carry the scent of wild
flowers,
or how it is even possible to be on your way back,
when you have only just discovered,
the reason for going forward at all.

The Problem(S) With 'Working Motherhood'

Working motherhood is such a complex and emotive subject to write about. Far more emotive than I ever realised prior to becoming a mother myself. It also took me a long time to understand that even the titles we use to describe motherhood and work are problematic in themselves, all mothers are working mothers, it's just that only some work is valued and paid. Setting these two roles up as competing binary opposites benefits only the patriarchy.

The fact that our culture and government (in the UK and the US particularly) doesn't value caring as highly as cash is something I regularly struggle with. Likewise, I believe that economic power is crucial for women's development and progress.

Choice, as always, is key. The lack of decent childcare infrastructure (the UK has the second most expensive childcare system in the world[*]), the gender pay gap[**] and many other inequalities mean that the word 'choice' is currently loaded, and the

---

[*]   https://stats.oecd.org/Index.aspx?DataSetCode=NCC

[**]   https://www.ons.gov.uk/employmentandlabour-market/peopleinwork/earningsandworkinghours/bulletins/genderpaygapintheuk/2020

word 'compromise' feels more appropriate. We need women to be able to more easily return to work after having a family and be paid fairly, just as we need men to be able to and want to stay at home and be valued highly.

In my experience, having done both, the sacrifices, challenges, stigma, rewards, fulfilment and joys weren't that dissimilar. The guilt was no less, or more, broadly our children appeared no more or less happy. Notably, I use the word 'appeared' here, because how could I ever really know? Perhaps child welfare doesn't feature highly enough in the debate, maybe because of the unspoken assumption that it is at the heart of everything we do. Or because I know that women are treated more harshly than men for daring to put our own needs higher up the agenda. Or even because, if I'm honest, I'm nervous that this gives traditionalists more ammunition to push women back into the kitchen. However, what I think IS interesting is switching the narrative to focus on the wealth of benefits that children gain from having a father actively involved in their care, benefits that are both cognitive and social*. We need more men actively involved in the care of children, not just because it benefits women, but because it benefits everyone.

---

* https://www.telegraph.co.uk/education/3110360/ Children-who-spend-time-with-their-fathers-have-a-higher-IQ.html

It still stings to recall the family member who questioned why I wouldn't just "be a mum" because I was returning to work (?) and likewise frustrates me that I struggle to describe the time I spent running a household and raising a family full-time as 'work'. As the parent who returned to work part-time after our first, I retained a lot of the domestic load and these routines became the norm. My husband and I have a completely equal relationship on every level, he has since taken a year off parental leave to look after a subsequent baby (and still speaks of this as one of his happiest years), we have both worked part-time at various points over the past ten years and pass the baton regularly when it comes to our careers. But undoubtedly my career stalled quite badly after that first return, and as he continued to get promotions and pay rises I was left floundering with bosses who embraced flexible working only on paper and in a company with a culture of long hours and presenteeism.

I have worked with hundreds of women supporting returns to work, and so I know that they range from great to downright awful and illegal. My own were mixed. The first two were fairly straightforward and positive, though I quickly realised part-time equalled no promotions or credibility. Subsequently, I had a manager who I knew wanted me to either leave or work full-time, and it felt awful.

I did leave. For a long time afterwards, I felt ashamed and embarrassed. I thought because my heart wasn't in it any more that I must have deserved what happened. I've since understood that my heart wasn't in it because I had been slowly side-lined from a trajectory of high performance and career success to stagnation purely because I chose to procreate. Decisions had been made without me, for me. I'd been worn down, and the determined creative in me had started to look elsewhere. This does not mean that I deserved what happened. It means I had begun to protect myself from what I could see was happening.

The feelings of being lost, pushed out, gagged, frustrated, side-lined, exhausted trying to prove yourself all over again, are sadly too common. And not just in paid employment, freelancers, business owners, the list goes on, struggling with the same concept. Mothers are seen as easy prey for pyramid selling schemes and end up doing jobs for which they are well over-qualified just to get the flexibility they need.

Too often we are left trying to fit ourselves into a working structure that is fundamentally flawed and then blaming ourselves for struggling to hold it all together. In her book, The Motherhood Penalty*, Joeli Brearley (founder of the brilliant charity Pregnant then Screwed) documents this in

---

*   https://pregnantthenscrewed.com/

exceptional detail. "When we asked, 'Can women have it all?" she says, "we didn't mean, 'Can women do it all?' which appears to be where we've ended up".

And here we move onto the double workload, because on top of all this, the majority of women are still running households. A 2019 study by University College London[*] found that less than 7% of couples share housework equally. A few can afford nannies to help out, but most cannot. A few have genuinely equal relationships where everything is shared, but again, too many do not. The double workload is a real problem— an elephant in the room and another stumbling block for feminism. More women are working, but at what cost to our mental and physical health?

Eliane Glaser[**], author of, 'Motherhood: A Manifesto' writes, "Mothers are still underpaid, overworked, exploited, overlooked, frazzled, isolated and perpetually guilty".
I think she is right!

We require a complete cultural shift in how we approach caring, more businesses who are genuinely good on flexible working, properly

---

[*]   https://www.ucl.ac.uk/news/2019/jul/less-7-couples-share-housework-equally
[**]   https://www.theguardian.com/lifeandstyle/2021/may/18/parent-trap-why-the-cult-of-the-perfect-mother-has-to-end

paid parental leave, fathers taking this leave, ring-fencing shared leave would help, properly subsidised childcare, improved healthcare support for the whole pregnancy / birth / postnatal period, the list goes on. These are the things that I think will allow us to move towards a genuinely fair, a kinder and more progressive parenthood and society.

I've painted a pretty grim picture here, and I'm unapologetic about that because I think it is important to acknowledge the realities, but I know that it isn't the case for everyone. There are some wonderful success stories, there are great employers out there, there are plenty of women who have gone on to run their own businesses and build empires and do work they love in a way that works after having children.

But the fact remains, 'working motherhood' is for too many a double-edged sword and change is so urgently needed before we are left to fall upon it.

Damned If You Do

"You're back. Great, how are you? Did you see we have that meeting at four? Things are crazy busy – hope you won't now be having to run out the door. Good to have you back, we've missed you, so relieved you're doing the same hours as before, did I mention we're busy? Got that big meeting at four."

"You've returned to work already, wow, that's, well— amazing. It wouldn't be for me, but it's obviously OK for you, your baby must be more settled, mine needs me though you see. You know that research on attachment, I'm sure you've read it through, but, you know perhaps going back so early, well it just feels right to you. Yours must be more resilient, used to being left, sorry, looked after by other people, maybe that's what they're used to."

"You're back, great, let's hit the ground running. There's money to be made, a jobs list to get through, did I mention the meeting at four, people to see, people to be paid. Nothing has changed, yeah, you won't be one of those. I heard of one in a different team, wanting new days, to work in different ways, let's just stick to getting some work done I say.
Are you OK by the way?"

"You're going back now, but won't you miss her? Who

will be at home? Your boss must be great to allow you that time, aren't you lucky, I didn't have that with mine. But you've always been ambitious, for me, I'm about family, I like to be near home because that matters to me, you see. I guess you must be really strapped, there's no other way, else why would you do it. Are you OK by the way?"

My friend, you have no idea the fear that is being held between your fingers, the times that you are standing in the middle of the road and blocking a full load that belongs to you.

When I back you we can move miles, but when you back yourself you will move mountains, and then you will see the light has been waiting for you all along,
and we will watch the sun rise *together.*

The Load

Jane was an undiagnosed carrier. She spent all of her days carrying, mainly, the weight of her dead mother's shortcomings. Boiled up with some of her own, as is the way, steadily stewed like sour apples carrying a discrete bitterness beneath rosy skin. Her determined friend Rachel, meanwhile, laden with numerous offspring, still carried the award for Employee of the Year 2010— which she never got round to winning. Marta, another of their close-knit group, was the most generous of the women. She carried a bag for life full of hopes and dreams for her two adored children, her precious load protected in no small part by its being wrapped in her own favourite angora cardigan. Sarah would raise her eyes at this, unobserved with melons stacked up past her eyeballs, cartons of milk tucked under both arms, eggs wedged precariously between aching thighs, bread squished under her chin on boxes of sugary cereal, which she knew was no good; blocking her view up the hill she had to climb daily. Sometimes she would smile and acknowledge the offer of help when her husband looked up in time to see her stagger in to the front door. Zelda's load was also largely her husband's doing behind closed doors, though that was never spoken about, and she, herself, would not acknowledge this fact until later, if indeed ever. Sara, at 15 the youngest of the group, would run past Zelda's immaculate house most mornings and wave if it was light, her fingers clenching only her knuckles after dark. Those who knew would detect a reduction in her movements now that she carried a male gaze, the carpet of hair on her arm pits untrodden, yet brushed with disgust. Baljit, meanwhile, faced the opposite end of this weight, carting around the disappearance of her own blood. Baljit, oh, Baljit, would now carry her own self mostly, thick layers of it leaving no room for much else of interest. Likewise, Evelyn would carry borrowed venom, steadily balancing a coffee cup in one hand, and a bag of hungry shame-ridden snakes in the other, tongues stabbing as they'd coil themselves up and round the handle and along her youthful arms towards her heart.

The others would offer their sympathies, their own nagging scars still itchy and raw.

These women, stoically working their ways through life. See these women, carrying the weight of a world too afraid to carry its own true weight.

See these women.

My Final Non-Return To Work Was All About Semantics:

What difference does it make to say, "if" she returns rather than "when"?
Just four solitary letters. Doesn't mean anything.

There was a particular keenness on the word "if" all round that day, though.
"If" I'd only...

(that promotion would be mine, I could do the same job, I'd not be forced out the door)

Or how about the word "able" as opposed to "un able"?
Just two letters there. Hardly worth mentioning.

I held more than two letters in my head, though, as I retreated to the car, avoiding eye contact with anyone on the stairs.

When in the meeting, I tried to argue the conversation we'd had weeks before,
"It's all semantics" you'd reply.

I wasn't sure whether you understood the meaning of the word, or understood it too well.

When the *verbatim* notes I then signed as an
accurate representation of the meeting were
without full paragraphs of our conversation, I just
sighed.

Oh, I understood alright,
whole generations of women held back
by *semantics.*

The Parental Game of Time

Welcome to the game of time: a game that is all about numbers and never about winning.

Well it is about winning, but, well, you won't. You'll make numerous incorrect moves whilst attempting to play the game right, like allocating 15 minutes to making a meal and clearing up the box of Lego that has been quite literally thrown across the room before realising you've actually used twenty-five minutes (damn you Jamie Oliver), which will then mess up the subsequent ten minutes you've allocated to the guilt-appeasing school reading (yep, ten was already ambitious) which then, consequently, messes up your whole. sodding. night.

Welcome to the game of time, where from now on every minute and every second, in fact every single breath, will be segmented and specified a slot. You'll secretly plan your days out by the hour. If you hit the park in the morning that will take you up to 12 p.m. Then you can justify a film at 3 p.m which will kill an afternoon. Then it will be on to sorting tea before it's the bedtime routine and then, 'wine time' (you won't actually say 'wine time,' though, because then you'd have no friends). And you won't actually admit to counting down to bedtime because then someone might suggest you are a bad parent, so you just keep this knowledge safely where we all keep it, in our heads.

Welcome to the game of time, where unfortunately you will need to learn to steal to survive. You see, there aren't enough hours in a day to play with, so you have to think sly like a fox. Stealthily swipe the odd 10 minutes, claim a dodgy meal the night before for an extra-long poo, a longer than expected work call or just hope it will go unnoticed (it never does, that's not how the game works, the time is added up and packed into a box marked resentment).

Welcome to the game of time. You'll need to learn to squeeze your days into a to-do list format. You'll have to number your daily actions (no logical order required, feel free to prioritise shopping over sleep) and allocate your time out accordingly. Here you'll enter the seedy world of time trades. Undercover, dirty, swaps. Like a 5 p.m. shift for a 7 p.m. one (because you know 4 p.m. is a right shitter, so you've got good bargaining power, but 7 p.m. allows you to sneak an early exit to the pub - where dreams are made).

Welcome to the game of time. Sadly, the instructions got chucked out after someone decided they knew the rules already. A man, probably, so don't be surprised if the cards aren't dealt out equally. Your husband's commitments are the Mayfair and Park Lane, where you'll be lucky to hold one of the pinks. Advance to the nearest male-owned property, do not pass go, do not collect £200, yes I know it would seem fair that everyone collected the same, but you're a woman, so you only get £150, just be grateful you've been allowed to play at all, alright?

Welcome to the game of time, where you (very) occasionally will get some for free, so DON'T mess it up by not using it wisely. The weak will panic when faced with an hour of untethered freedom, but you should know that no strings attached isn't a thing, your hour 'off' sits tempting you to relax but whatever you do you'll regret it because the washing pile won't sort itself, so grab your phone and give your mum a ring (because you haven't had time for this all week I bet) and attempt to fit in everything that you didn't get round to last week, and everything you know needs urgently doing this week into this single precious hour slot. Good luck with that.

Welcome to the game of time. You might want to stop playing at some point but sadly by the time you realise this, you'll be too damn tired to do anything about it, not to mention that everyone else is playing, and you don't want to be 'that guy.' Find five minutes you can meditate, five minutes for some yoga (add one or two minutes to feel smug for worthy time choices), give twenty away unknowingly to people you don't know on Twitter (feel a bit less smug) and then add on another twenty-five minutes to read a chapter of a new book that claims to help you find more time to live (and if it works, let me know).

It Was Never About The Braiding

Sometimes she will say no.
Shoulder my arm away
and my husband will say:

"Why don't you just let her shove it in a ponytail?"

But what would be the good in that,
when I have scrunchies at the ready like rainbows,
and can remove the broken bobby pins,
attempt to click back the click-clacks with one
hand.

You see, there are some people who can't plait,
but I am not one of them.
This, at least, I can do perfectly.

Guilt Pie

When I had my first baby, I wasn't sure I wanted
pie.
But I was served some anyway.
As I cradled her head, warm and smelling of joy,
someone walked in, brazen, and popped a slice on
the birth plan notes by my bed.
Meat and potato, fresh from the oven.
The women on my ward also thought it was a
bit crazy, but the bounty lady circled dishing out
good mum gravy and there was even cherry pie for
dessert, with 'breast is best' ice cream.
So I took a bite to eat, just to try and at least show
I was keen.
I don't even eat meat.

In the weeks that followed, I began to see guilt pie
everywhere.
Offered up with cups of tea by well-meaning
health visitors.
Large slabs adding an obsession with weight onto
my plate.
Ads for a really great gluten-free sausage plait on
the telly in-between episodes of Homes Under
The Hammer so as I sat in my jammies watching
Maxine from Bury make 20k from a total wreck
of a flat (again) the smell of pie would hit me in
the face, and it's all I would think about for hours.
You'll eat anything if you're hungry enough.
Guiltily gobble it up.

As the months moved on, pie throwing became a
bit of a hobby for those of us living on two hours'
sleep and a rich tea because by now most of my
mum mates had far too much pie to keep. We'd
had pies posted through our letterboxes, posted on
our phones, posted into our mouths as we opened
them to say, "We're a bit full actually, thanks."
When your little beauty is up all night, it's quite
hard to manage the fruity little number on your
bedside table made with apples that should only
be sliced a very specific way (definitely not the way
you're doing it, in case you were wondering).
So we'd offer Suzy, who hadn't done any baby
classes whatsoever, (!) a small slice of chicken and
mushroom. She'd politely decline (bloody Suzy,
always letting the side down) so we'd pop them
in her bag for later when she was alone and got
peckish.
She'd eat it.

I thought when I went back to work, I could have
a break from guilt pie.
People said that you drink hot tea and go to the
toilet on your own, so surely
I could leave my pie at home and get a nice salad
sandwich instead.
Turns out there were just more flavours of pie to
try.
I could pick up a shepherd's "shouldn't you be at
home being a mum" pie at any point.
My boss kept a stash of mini pork pies (obviously
there was some pie policy somewhere which
stated that this not a REAL pie) which they'd pop

onto my desk on the days I wasn't in so the smell
of stale meat would be lingering for when I came
back and could put them in the bin (bastard).
To be fair, some days I did manage to forget about
pie.
Then there'd be a meeting that was so important,
so urgent, so inflexible, that I couldn't miss
without letting down the entire team, the entire
company, the entire universe, so I'd grab a handful
of those little porkie numbers and nip to the loo.
Game over.

It's taken me an age, but I've finally realised that
all these guilt pies (and others I can't even begin
to list on this page) are not mine, even though I've
bought them and eaten them and thought about
them all the time. That the only thing to do is to
wipe my mouth and wash my hands and refuse to
buy the pies (even, especially, if you see a stunning
new recipe on Twitter that you want to try on for
size).
And the pie-makers, well they'll panic because
they need us to keep buying the pies for them
to survive, and they'll start stacking the pies
outside our doors, so we can't get out the house
and so high that they reach our windows making
it almost impossible for us to see beyond the
pastry tops and the friendly fillings and the lovely
homely, welcoming smell we know so well whilst
pies masquerading as pasties marketed as vegan
and definitely containing "no dangerous nasties"
pepper the lawn.

But they can't make us eat their pies, stodgy and too filling and laced with lies.
We can gather them up, and we can let them go cold. We can encourage each other to shop elsewhere and chuck them in the bin, return them to all the people and places that they came from. Then choose to have pie on the odd Sunday, perhaps an occasional mid-week supper on a Monday so that lighter, with two hands and clearer heads, we can get back to what we were meant to be doing.

Pie free.

Dear fellow mothers,

When you can't make the figures add up, when you look at your childcare bills and feel like a bad feminist for wondering whether it's actually worth working at all.

Not your fault.

When you get home but still check your emails because, despite working many more than your paid hours without so much as a lunch break, your boss doubts your commitment, especially if you work flexibly.

Not your fault.

When you fall into bed exhausted every night because for some reason you're the only one who knows how to work the washing machine and do the online food shop and find an outfit for the school play.

Not your fault.

When you doubt every decision you make, feel guilty for working, guilty for not working, guilty for taking any time off even though you really just need something for yourself.

None of this is your fault.

You are doing your best within a society that is not set up for mothers, a world that is not kind to women full stop.

Do not take responsibility for a problem that you didn't create, it is a heavy load which you do not deserve to carry, and it will drag you down.

This shame is not yours.

None of this is your fault.

You, my friend, are not broken.

The system is broken.

You are an absolute

Rock star.

Quantifiable

I've lost count of the number of school runs and
drop-offs, so I couldn't hand you a figure now,
even if you asked. The first birthday party was
noted somewhere, but after that—

the amount of beds I've changed won't fit into
the cards you might write me, so I wouldn't even
attempt to carry the clothes I've washed in one set
of arms, all the meals I've cooked lying beneath
ironed shirts—

and the teeth and knees and mouths and bums and
shoes and sides and toilets and floors I've cleaned
will no longer fit within these walls, so I'll stack
them by the front door

where I hope you'll trip over them on your return
home.

Five

Hold On

There is despair.

Because women were already dodging burnout before 2020, already fighting to level the playing field, already exhausted by the work that needs to be done as fires burn down forests and fear pushes people apart.

There is hope.

Because just as the sun rises and sets each day, mostly without anyone declaring its brilliance, we'll continue to rub cold toes and pop food into small mouths, we'll continue to hold out our arms and look both ways, we'll continue to craft stories with hopeful endings because we are well acquainted with the type of love that will save us all.

Love, that will save us all.

In 2020. In This Park.

I've watched my baby turn into a toddler in this park.
I've seen my children learn how to ride bikes
in this park.
I've felt the deepest exhaustion blur my eyes
in this park.
I've seen other parents learning how to survive
in this park.
I've ticked the box on the list marked exercise
in this park.
I've cried hot tears of anger and frustration
in this park.
I've wiped them swiftly on my sleeve and kept on
walking in this park.
I've witnessed true kindness in strangers faces
in this park.
I've spent surprisingly long times in old but new
places in this park.
I've had weary, cloudy days which went on forever
in this park.
I've turned casual hellos into beautiful friendships
in this park.
I've sprinkled words into gaps on cold benches
in this park.
I've stood on that spot over there in every type of
weather in this park.
I've drunk weak tea out of a crappy flask in this park.
I've laughed and laughed until I needed a wee
in this park.
I've drunk mulled wine out of the same flask in this

park (hence the above).
I've questioned what the hell it is I'm doing
in this park.
I've known when a hand has lifted my children up
in this park.
I've told stories and held out my arms to catch
stories in this park.
I've served drinks and dealt with tricky customers
in this park.
I've offered up biscuits and the contents of the
bottom of my bag in this park .
I've wiped noses and eyes and so much dirt off
random limbs in this park.
I've learnt to listen to each new season's rhythms
in this park.
I've discovered that gates are only closed until
they are opened in this park.
I've followed my children trudging up the hills of
alright in this park.
I've held my children as we've swung from day to
night and back again in this park.
I've hoped to never have to return to this park.
I've pleaded to go ANYWHERE else for a change
instead of this park.
And yet, my pockets are crammed with reminders
of all that we survived together.

In this park.

We Are Parents, This Is What We Do

The lake across town wasn't exactly where I wanted to be, and it's now the last place I ever want to visit again, but as we pulled into the car park that February afternoon, my enthusiasm grew. A late sun was setting beautifully across the water and within minutes the kids, all but my two-year-old, were trying, and failing, to break ice using large sticks.

We were all letting off steam, releasing our pent-up frustration after yet another week of forced homeschooling during a pandemic. Finally, they were free to roam, their laughter mimicking the cool sharp light bouncing up off the glassy surface as we began our walk.

We'd taken the pram *(thank god)* which led to an interesting moment early on as we negotiated crossing some stepping stones. The two oldest, at ten and eight, were giddy at the challenge of dragging a strong-willed toddler across some slightly innocuous looking water. The six-year-old less so, which just added to the heady thrill for everyone else.

Despite the wind brushing like sandpaper against our cheeks, it was all going so much better than I'd imagined when I left the house an hour earlier, hoping to kill a bit of time at the end of a long week. The kids were collecting minibeasts, singing songs and holding hands unprompted. There were smiles of admiration from chatty fellow walkers. There was a giddy, playful freedom in the air which I tried to capture on my phone but couldn't, despite numerous attempts.

Here I was, winning at parenting. Ticking off the boxes on the vigorous perfect mother checklist which we all keep in our back pocket. Suddenly a distinctly average lake is resembling Lake Garda, and I'm preparing to accept my Mother of the Year award. In my head the kids are shouting: "Mummy you are the best, we love you because you are such a fun, relaxed, adventurous parent". So I think it's understandable that I made the decision for us to keep going all the way round, despite knowing that we'd done barely a quarter of the route. My husband would never have made this decision, but then he could take or leave said parenting award.

And for about another fifteen minutes or so, this decision was completely valid. Until the first complained of being hungry, and the sentiment spread like wildfire. Now I had snacks, of course I had, this was not my first rodeo, but all parents know that when to bring out the snacks is a big decision. A game changer, if you will. It's the parenting equivalent of a game of poker. You have half decent cards, you feel fairly confident, but you have to read the room and hold your nerve. Go too early, and you'll be regretting it for the rest of the trip. Go too late and no matter what you pull out will be met with pure white anger.

The snacks I had brought were Soreen bars. Not the least popular item, it wasn't fruit - which may well have seen me lynched, but certainly not something that would guarantee me an all-out win. Let's just say I was already keenly aware that I should have sneaked in a pack of biscuits. I needed to be strategic, and a bird-watching hut around the next bend felt like a good target. Unfortunately, the toddler was insisting on being out of said pram, so 50 yards was looking like a ten-minute battle. The six-year-old had now insisted on sitting in the way-too-small pram, making it sway and struggle precariously over the frozen mud. The signs were written right across the cold ground.

Here I made my second parenting error.

In a bid to move things forward, I described the bird hut as some sort of Mecca-like-lake attraction; a bird-viewing haven. It was aimed mostly at the toddler, but the others were all ears with half the tolerance. I may (I did) have mentioned flamingos (!)

We've all done it, exaggerating comes with the

territory, so you'll know how this pans out. We get to the hut and about three miles away you can just about make out two of those ducks which you've seen on every pond in every park on every weekend over the past 12 months. Even the toddler doesn't give a shit about these ducks. And whilst I try to point out non-existent birds with names I can't even pronounce from the 'not useful information board' another mum with her son, brilliantly prepared in adequate clothing for the weather, rocks up sporting binoculars, sandwiches and a tolerance I'm not sure I ever owned. She didn't seem thrilled at the noise the toddler was now making, having wolfed his bar in two mouthfuls, and I wasn't keen on how the others were observing what a good job looked like, so we moved on. I basically promised Disney World and gave them Disneyland Paris, in winter, when none of the rides were open. An uprising was brewing and I knew it.

Assessing my options, I realised we were about halfway round. Turns out, lakes can be really deceptive. Should the walk have ended there, I'd say there would have been mixed reviews. I'd have lost a few marks due to the cold, but I might have scraped together a couple of good comments on account of the authorised ice smashing.

But the walk did not end there.
No, the walk was very much not over.

And since the options were to turn back or carry on, and since neither was shorter nor preferable, we trudged forward. At this point, I had to dig deep for back up. Stories made up off the top of my head gifted me ten minutes, a couple of swans bought me five, the odd 'race you' game gets the toddler back in the pram and the others covering more ground. The eight-year-old decides he can 'talk to geese' which I don't question and instead encourage because there are plenty to see IF WE KEEP GOING.

The trickle of other walkers had now become the odd guy walking a dangerous dog, it's bared teeth as off-putting as the vicious bite of the wind, attacking us face on. The last of the day's light is illuminating the other side of the lake like a stage, which I try to use as a distraction, I'm keen to demonstrate our progress and recall happier times. They barely look up, feet shuffling, muttering disdain.

The second youngest has now begun to cry. This is not good, the car is still nowhere in sight and I can't listen in to her tears because they reflect the uncomfortable truth of my own inadequacies. The sound is only half audible anyway over the noise of the M60, which apparently passes pretty close to this section of our scenic walk. Even the toddler has started complaining that his toes are sore, which I know is probably true, but without any hope of a resolution I pretend I haven't heard him either. I wonder if my cold response to their needs

reflects a lack of care, when in reality the care is
so great I fear it will overwhelm me if given space
to breathe.

And then the goose whisperer arrives at my side,
keen to discuss a handful of litter he has rescued
from the lake. *That's right*, he is now handing
me wet litter. I have zero resolve as he pushes
a crushed lager can and some slimy plastic into
my pocket. The eldest meanwhile, designated (by
me) second carer, is trying to console her little
sister whilst the toddler, the sturdiest of the lot,
continues to stagger with an unwieldy stick that I
daren't take off him despite the fact it is regularly
threatening to add another blow to proceedings.
The whole situation is dire, and I swing from
angry (at myself and motherhood and life) to
sugary sweet with guilt and then back again.

I throw a bit of bribery and manipulation in
for good measure, I sing the odd slightly manic
sounding song, I remember something I read
somewhere about vulnerability and try to describe
my own emotional state, though a watered down
version because no-one needs those future therapy
bills. I forget that kids taste emotions better than
any therapist, and they spit the fake positivity
I'm feeding them right back into my weary arms.
My enthusiasm is as volatile as my perception of
myself as a mother, and the question of, "why can't
we just go for a walk without it being this hard?"
is on repeat in my brain.

I decide the only option is to take charge and apply the *'stride forward with purpose, and they will follow'* technique, so by now I am at least three metres ahead, driving the pram into the wind (somehow again pushing the second youngest too-big child after she rose to my stage analogy, and lay on the floor arms spread announcing that "she simply could not go on"), shouting clichéd phrases like a win-obsessed American soccer coach— which is only serving to irritate everyone including myself. Of course, I end up stopping to wait for them to catch up. But you knew this. Obviously, I also then end up carrying a stickless, hysterical toddler whilst trying to push a pram with handles weighed down by shiny images of other peoples' children behaving impeccably and Friday nights in beer gardens. And the easy eight-year-old ends up carrying his older sister on his back, you know you're in trouble when her good nature is blown.

On any other day, this would be funny. In fact now, in hindsight, I can see that it was a comical scene as we staggered around the last corner towards a now almost empty car park, with three out of four kids (and almost one adult) crying and me STILL insisting that we'd had "a really lovely time" because that parenting award was so damn shiny, and I did not have nearly enough time to show I deserved it.

In the car, heaters blasting, I call my husband, who

I realise will be getting concerned after our 'quick walk' has turned into a three-hour night trek. He suggests pizza, he can order, and we can collect it on our way home, a Friday night treat.

He wins parent of the year.

And in this instant, everything is good. The kids rejoice at this news and instantly forget about the last few hours. And I admit that this wasn't the best walk, but point out that we all survived and the eldest squeezes my hand and reassures me that it wasn't so bad, and the middle two are playing a game with a smaller stick they've rescued which is making the toddler roar with laughter, and I don't care if they ever know the names of fancy birds. My shoulders begin to return to their rightful place and I remove my coat, but keep it nearby even as my anxiety thaws because I have been a parent long enough to know that the weather is consistently changeable.

That you'll enjoy stretches of time with a good tailwind, when a small, warm hand will sneak into yours, and you'll laugh about the whole world they've imagined happening beneath the murky water, followed by others when weariness seeps into your bones and neediness prickles your eyes and discover that both are completely normal and that it will all probably be OK in the end.

Years of trying to shake the mistaken belief that

you are entirely responsible for your offspring's happiness, to limit the resulting pressure to perform your part at all times because the one giving out the awards definitely doesn't have your best interests at heart, or they'd have changed the winning criteria centuries ago. Allowing the opportunities to learn and see each icy lake more clearly to be synonymous with the challenge of not losing yourself and discovering your own unique place in the world.

That there will be times when you think you can't go on and then turn the corner or ask for help and find the strength to go again, without stopping to consider how much it means in doing so. The fact that you have no choice but to go again because you've fallen so deeply in love.

Because we are parents, and *this* is what we do.

Progress Isn't Permanent

There was no large scale robbery,
no newsworthy event to speak of.
No dates were written in the history books for
future students to ponder,
the girls taking longer to formulate an opinion—
if permitted to speak at all.

Perhaps that's why they can be forgiven for failing
to notice.
A plague masked the signs, of course.
The pack of dogs dined well, having exhausted
their prey.
Divided up those who remained to breathe
another day.

No, the fallback was more like a dripping tap.
Crucial bodies smuggled into suitcases.
The gradual snatching away of choices.
Discrete scratching of open wounds and cutting
out of voices.

But perhaps it is fair to ask the question:
"Did they cling more tightly to their phones than
their rights?"
And was there too much time spent looking for
the right traps,
as the rats slept comfortably in their own beds at
night?

It Could Be Worse

"It could be worse," said the man at the park,
"we would play on bomb sites as kids, nothing like
this."

"Yes, it could be worse," said the girl at the
swings,
mouth suddenly dry and empty, swallowed
frowning

and yet–

you can look gratitude in the eye whilst speaking
of how
your days are so long.

You can long for a taste of normal, knowing that
normal could taste sour,
feel spread too thin.

You can feel drenched by the rain, cold rage
beneath your skin and still
want to look up and see the rainbow.

It could be worse,

and also—

it could be better.

We would break,
if only there were some place
for the pieces to land.

A Poem That Has Nothing To Do With Luck

I remain up tonight.
Sit at the top of the stairs waiting.
We've drunk in all our love for each other
and I am still swimming in it.
Still smiling about a story you told too loud,
can still smell the fried food on my clothes.
And it is late, and I've got to be up early, but on I
will wait,
take off my bracelets,
flick through my phone,
try not to think how I'd describe the colour of your
coat
as my heart hovers above the pit of my stomach
waiting for a text to tell me that you are home.
And I will regret not forcing you into that taxi,
and perhaps forcing you into that taxi.
My head heavy now against the wall
staring at the still open door to my right -
the landing light kept on (for now),
and I know that I have a lot of waiting left inside
me.
Then in a flash, tonight we become the lucky ones.
Who get to undress our own bodies.
Who get to brush our teeth and think
about whether there's milk for the morning.
Who get to make it into bed.
But who can not for one. single. second
forget.

Rising Wild

Can we run around naked?
Can I play in bare feet?
Can we start the day when,
I've had enough sleep?

Can I try and learn it this way,
even though it makes a mess?
Can I paint my nails all colours,
and fight pirates in a dress?

Can I sit down when I want to,
even though we're on the go?
Can I keep moving when I need to,
and jump and twirl and throw?

Can I eat when I am hungry?
Can we have a break from time?
Can I have the space to take a risk,
and not fall out of line?

Can we sing songs to the clouds?
Can I explore that long-lost day?
Can it be OK to be myself,
and just allowed to play?

Of course you can, my babies.
I'll stand back, let you run wild.
Here's the freedom that you never should have lost
when just a child.

Motherhood Minus the Medals

I want a medal and I want one for my mates too, and the woman I saw in the park pushing a pram with spreadsheets behind her eyes and a 'too long now' weariness in her bones. I want one for the other I know sweats through a Zoom call watching the clock for the end of the TV programme she has lined up (for the third time that day). Like it's a ticking career time bomb, feeling "grateful" not to be one of the others on Instagram describing how they knew it would be redundancy all along.

I want medals hanging heavy off yielding trees, so we have to duck our heads as we chase the little feet we are protecting with our every breath. I want them strewn across every inch of our homes, so that as we move from worker to carer to partner to friend to worker again, laden with freezer food and flash wipes, we feel their metal; keen cold reminders that we are worthy winners. I want them nestled in a metal chest hidden away from greedy blue fingers, protecting only those with big talk and fast cars.

I want medals hanging proudly off every neck celebrating that we've won gold in the 'just getting through the day" Olympics. That we've swum through treacle and jumped through hoops that

were too high off the ground and raced against
time to get the odd worksheet done to appease
our guilt. I want medals hanging off all our necks
as we crawl deliberately around the supermarket,
enjoying half an hour of what is now known
as a break, lingering longer than necessary but
enjoying the experience less because borrowed
time is a feeling that's hard to shake.

I want a medal, for the exhaustion and the losses,
for doing more than our bit. I want medals that
glimmer for longer than a day, that once given
out aren't crammed into dark corners of musty
drawers that we end up rooting through looking
for scraps of our mental health. But here, the ones
giving out the gold don't actually give a shit. We're
the foot soldiers, collateral damage, they know
we'll take a hit because we love hard and have long
been fighting for our place, which is tough when
we can't actually think straight or find time to
even sit.

I want a medal.
We all deserve so much more than a medal.
Where are all the medals?

Hug

I really want to hug you,
properly.
Not a brief, fleeting sort of hug,
a bit too polite
like a lukewarm cup of tea
just shown the bag,
hardly worth the effort.
No, not one of those.

I want the hot sponge pudding
with thick velvety custard sort of hug.
A gluttonous hug,
which overflows from the bowl.

One which melts our middles.
One which clings to our bones.
One which moulds our moods
as a candle draws out the dark.

I really want to hug you,
desperately.
So that my mind
can reclaim your shape
and incubate the endorphins
for darker days.
Wrap them up
somewhere soft,
somewhere safe.

A hug that only gets better with time
our arms eventually growing old together with
grace
A full on hug which doesn't fear the future cold
space.

One which feels like everything
I didn't say and everything I ever could.

One which reminds me that I exist.
One which tastes like home.

Headspace

I have no space in my head.

I feel a bit like Jack Bauer, but instead of 24 hours, I've got about five and instead of a made-up world which has all gone wrong I'm trying to survive in my own house. I hide in the bathroom with my weapon of a toothbrush, which I use for far too long just to be by myself, lock the door, hear someone shout that the baby has chucked cereal all over the floor. I'm knee-deep in this impossible mission which we all said couldn't be done, but the control room wouldn't listen or didn't care, and my own version of a countdown to bedtime begins in my head (it's 6 a.m.) and I realise that I've already spent far too long dragging out this analogy because, quite frankly, it is easier than trying to articulate reality which is exactly what happens when you

have no space in your head

and the workload keeps coming, and I keep catching it and catching it, high catches, low catches, those where you have to be running which is fine because I am, obviously. And at first I use my hands and my arms and then hang some guilt around my neck for the bits that I've skipped and stuff some deadline fear into my pockets, you know, whilst I'm here, and when I used up all my

body parts I start on the kitchen sides and under
the sofas and down the back of chairs. Maths sums
slip out from under the rug as I'm trying to change
a nappy as lost logins land on my plate while I'm
trying to eat a sandwich as an email holds out its
hands to be held as I'm trying to make tea as a
phone call I forgot to make nudges me to move up
in the middle of the night, and I am obsessed with
trying to make sure my kids are vaguely happy
meaning

I have no space in my head

to sort anything into any kind of order, the filing
cupboard of my mind needs a major rearrange, but
just as I start to be less of a worry hoarder there's
yet another change. The shelves are no longer
large enough to fit all the schedules— hang on
when did anyone last eat any vegetables? The
walls are groaning, the days all confused, I've lost
the drawer marked priorities, no idea when our
toddler last got new shoes. And yet the weekends
are empty, maybe right now should feel quiet
and yet somehow it feels like I'm orchestrating a
riot of rage in my head and I long for outside, a
break from hearing my own name, never imagined
loving like I do now the feel of cold, winter
rain, hold my arms out and spin, legs loosening
the knots within, where I won't bump against
anything or anyone which is a small victory when
there is

no space in my head

for the projects I crave and the rest that I need
and I know that my chat tastes like the dregs of
weak tea, if I don't ask about your day it's because
I am running on empty, not because I don't care,
not because I'm being rude, I know it's hard to
anticipate dips on this rollercoaster of mood. But
with this last hour to go, it's gone right to the
wire, and we need to save ourselves, so we can
save others from the fire, so excuse yourself and
leave the room, if you literally can't face one more
painfully bad Zoom, if you need to lose yourself in
books, or food, or dance, or whatever it takes, if
you're still these wearing those filthy sweatpants,
that you can't make decisions, go straight to bed
at eight, you're bloody exhausted, the jobs' list can
wait while we all do whatever is required to find

the space we need for our heads.

Nelly Bryce

Less Snatched Moments

Give me endless fields where green thoughts can
grow into revolutions.
Let me see the future in the distance, with a
lifetime in my legs to wander,
so that I can lie on the grass with mindless
minutes dancing around my fingertips,
and the days dangling lazily in the breeze.

Mother Earth

I wonder will she laugh loudly enough to hear as
we beg,
like a child, pretending not to have heard the word
stop
as we race recklessly towards the swings,
feet falling faster than legs.

I wonder are the trees whispering behind our
backs?
Roots huddled round
drinking dark caffeine riddled coffee
Rotting sugar-free.

I wonder whose job it will be to nail the coffin?
Mute well-wishers recalling brighter times,
as (first) the heels of their carefully chosen shoes,
sink beneath the salty surface.

I wonder will the Polaroid be in black and white,
that she holds up to her friends
Will she wonder if there is anything to be learnt
from losing a child this way.

Nelly Bryce

The Recovery Lounge

I saw us at the park this week.
Sky full of dirty clouds,
the sound of scooters being scraped across
gravelly windswept ground,
weighing up activities on the wellbeing scales we
now store heavily in our heads,
wiping knees muddy as our moods.

Broken mirrors reflecting smiles strung so tightly
they might snap,
a weariness threading its way round the swings,
up the ramp, and back.
Our conversations brief and tilted,
time bound like the kid hovering on the top stair
of the slide,
taking up room in the small places that are
allowed to be occupied.
And there aren't many to find.

Our minds being held together with sticky tape
which lost its hold months ago.
The same questions now feeling age-old:
Fine. Alright. Getting there.
Getting where, I wonder,
all the walking.
Same park, same pavements, same faces.
Same policies, same leaders, same spaces.
Feels so short on destinations right now, this path,
carrying and carving up time into tiny pieces of

play,
dragging out limbs for fresh air purely for the
chance to say,
OK screens on, eyes down, we've made it through
another day.

Perhaps we could end up some place soon?
Shall I make us a hot coffee?
Steal some keys to a secret room
where we are all welcome to stay,
filled with feather pillows and arm strokes and
a year's-worth of sleep tied up in bows by our
beds.
Days of pointless television and hot buttered toast
which tastes exactly like it did,
you know,
when it felt like we could do anything.

And it will be all slipper socks and jammies with
fleecy tops
as we finally take off the needs of others worn so
tightly on our chests.
Step out of expectations and brave a proper rest,
curl up together and hibernate and recover in the
ways that we know best.

Lie still for as long as we need,
fill our too tense lungs with gulps of anxiety-free
air,
lift our heads, let down our hair, liberate our eyes
from their lookouts
to see shafts of light landing on fresh sheets.
And we will feel held, by ourselves, by each other,

by those we love.
As we become ourselves again.
As mothers, as women, we will become more than
ourselves again.
And wouldn't this be a whole new sight?

Six

Imagine

Be the spark
The tiny flickering possibility
The stone dropped onto a tabletop lake
The nudge in the arm of a maybe
The mind that wonders
The hand that pulls out of a pocket
The fire it will burn
Be the spark

(for Louise, who knew before I did,
that I should write this book)

On Motherhood And Identity

Identity wise, I found becoming a mother profoundly unsettling.
The challenge, I now realise, is to resettle in a way that is led by you; that is purposeful and that holds meaning.

I did not manage this ten years ago after having my first baby. I was too scared and too fixated on returning to the normal I once knew, even though that normal wasn't something I couldn't remember ever actually choosing. Society does an excellent job of chastising mothers, who are expected to adhere to countless unwritten rules on everything from birth choices through to parenting styles. There's a very public commentary on 'poor parenting' alongside a quiet removal of decent support systems and structures. I found the pressure to conform to an idealised motherhood sat tidily behind comments from well-meaning friends, immaculate homes on social media and advice from professionals.

I was too keen to accommodate goals that were not my own and, probably, too well-trained to run off the lead. With a new tiny human being teaching me all over again how to live and play, it took more than a few years to recalibrate.

Though I realise now that a tiny crack had been forced during that very first maternity leave, and I started writing more consistently, something I hadn't done since a teenager, even throughout my English degree. Becoming a mother gave me permission to play, permission that too often isn't granted by a society which demands that we are defined by the hours we work and the money we make.

Working in HR, leadership development, I returned to the office championing time away from the office for our managers— in part to support good mental health, but also to inspire new thinking and creativity. I've never understood why a break on a CV is viewed as a bad thing. Why is it that we think human beings must work to the death, literally?

Aside from the many, many skills that mothers gain from keeping a small child alive (too many to mention here), just having that time away from the day job can bring renewed enthusiasm, new ideas and so much more. Just one of a stupendously long list of reasons why employers are crazy not to employ more mothers/support more parents to balance a family with a career/support more humans to have a life, and why I'd like to hope that having more women in senior positions could help make this shift happen. More women, that is, who are prepared to forge a new type of leadership and not just recreate the status quo.
And with subsequent children I got braver, I

went deeper, I started to mould my identity into something it perhaps always was, or perhaps something altogether new, and yet so much more familiar. The heady heights of success finally became for me entirely self-designed, which was a relief in that this also meant far less precarious.

Motherhood, with its tsunami of emotions and ever-long days and nights, creates the perfect conditions for reinvention. Even though, *especially though*, the obliteration of what came before can be terrifying. Although, of course, there is very little time for doing much during the early years, not to mention that sleep deprivation clouds your thinking and finances can be strained. But whilst already challenging every assumption you ever made about yourself and your life, it is not such a huge step to go further, reflecting on the routines that represent our truths, the causes that heighten our voices, and the experiences that bring us the most joy.

For me personally, influenced, but no longer solely driven by my work, with the work itself better reflecting my values, and encompassing more hobbies and projects and self-care and community into daily life, meant that with my fourth baby I felt more patient and calm about the inevitable identity loss; knowing that it wasn't identity loss at all, it was an identity holiday. A holiday from which I would return not exactly relaxed and bronzed but different, wiser, even more in love and perhaps even more myself.

Nelly Bryce

After An Unspecified Amount Of Time, I Call Out The Search Party

I pull out the mint green sewing machine
which I never did learn to use
Pass her a selection of pots and pans
from the kitchen drawer to play

My foot has begun to tap lightly
The next day it's my computer
I write and I write and I write
about her, our days, how I'm with her
and yet don't know how to be with her

She watches my fingers race with wonder
clenching and unclenching her own chubby fists
On the final day I bake
follow a recipe that feels like teaching myself to
read

She has discovered her voice
The house is filled with a scent I don't yet
recognise

When the friends I've only just met arrive later
laden with arm loads of babies—
squashy thighs spilling over strengthening biceps
they mistake the cakes I present as evidence
of my knowing who the hell I am any more.

When I Go To Say That I Am Just A Mother

I ask my daughter what she wants to be when she
grows up
I dislike the question, but I am interested in the
answer
She says that she just wants to be a mother

I urge her, but what else
encourage her to expand
that she *(that I)* can be more than *just a mother*
I list the other things that she could do as well as
this thing—
which is so beautiful
but not absolute
I tell her that she can have children to be a mother
or not
and also-

she ignores me
lists the children she will have
ten, twelve, maybe more
share them with her best friend
another fierce, gentle girl who she adores
(she ends, after another ten minutes musing, on
four)

And her face, it lights up
for she sees what too often I have lost sight

that she needs not to remove fences
because for her, they never existed
—and I might be a childminder, and a vet
and an Olympic gymnast
and I will look after you too
and we'll have dogs
and we'll all live together—

That she sees motherhood
in all its vivid colours
twirling it around in the air
and catching it, all ribbons and grins
pausing to demand heartfelt applause
stopping to take a bow

A motherhood not just of babies and vaginas
but relationships and care and love
with no limits as to who and with whom
No question of how
Yes, she sees motherhood

this six-year-old girl
teaching me
the gift of being a mother.

Imagining A Motherhood No Longer Wrapped In Cellophane On A Garage Forecourt

Imagine a world glistening with mothers. Where they grow wild on street corners and down shared walkways. Have roots in the centres of glass buildings, where they bloom and grow out loud— every breath more alive for their existence. Where we ask children to paint them in Spring, to capture their yellowy, youthful hopefulness. Then, when the daylight hours are longer, put them in vases centre stage on long tables to eat great food. If their bodies should fall to the ground; bruised perhaps from the harsher weather, imagine that we gather them up and stir them into potions, fill intoxicating glass bottles of blues, greens, pinks— colours that go far beyond what we assumed we knew, and for which people will queue for miles and miles, will beg to understand, appreciating that they are truly life-giving. Where we weave their fierceness into spiky cinnamon scented wreaths or dry them as their vibrancy fades but is no less beautiful, place them purposefully next to fireplaces, and on polished wooden dressers, where visitors will stop and stare, unable to pass by, oblivious.

Know that you can fall
That there will be
some words
someone has written
somewhere
that will catch you
and if by chance there aren't
that you can
write your own.

Spare Room

I can see now where the best place would be to
hang a mobile
There's a slight slant in the ceiling towards the far
wall
I've never noticed it before
Today, the light from the open window is
decorating it
It could be perfect

I don't suppose I've ever sat here at this time of
day
What is it, 3 p.m.?
The afternoon figures briefing will be happening
about now
He's right though, I mustn't think of that

My fingers fall to the neat stack of tiny folded
vests by my side
waiting patiently to be filled by somebody
Ironed into perfectly flat mirror images of each
other
Muted colours of beige and cream to match

My weights need to be moved out of here
Struggled to find a new home for them
They can't stay, of course
within these four empty walls
This large room waiting patiently to be filled with
life

They're just sat gathering dust in the corner
But that's not a job for me

Today my work is to prepare a set of drawers
and I will do so diligently
with the same attention to detail that I've always
had
He will laugh later
say something he thinks is funny about how I've
changed
and I will agree and find him a smile

The drawers are fuller than I anticipated
heavy with so much that's been collected over time
things unfit to display

I take a deep breath and consider putting this off
for another day
but the days feel limited now
so I start on the second drawer down, pulling
things out one by one
working methodically in this bid for space
The piles grow steadily around my still-skinny legs
Some start to encroach so
I reach over quickly to ensure separation
The smooth plastic of a breast pump feels alien in
my hand
like I've stolen someone else's belonging
My eyes scan the room guiltily
An attempt to steady myself

I think I hear the door
and wonder when the light changed

A duskiness has spread its way across the newly
fitted carpet
He insisted on only the softest wool
He'll come up and put his arms around my waist
I'll pretend to have just started
I've done a good job though
Box ticked, room fit for purpose

Study books, the pages still crisp, stacked for the
tip
Photo albums from before, unopened
I've been told pigment can be easily damaged by
light
Shoebox with its faded 90s font
An arm load of gig tickets, the first and the last
Other snippets of days that I must have felt worth
trying to remember

The parcel tape gets stuck to my fingers
as I struggle to fit the lid back on
But now the box sits neatly in the pile marked
'loft'
Still quiet rings out
Perhaps I was mistaken
Agitation stirs in my bones
One last sweep of the bottom drawer

And there it is
Untethered beneath a random old sock I don't
recognise
The taste of cheap, sweet alcohol
The smoke clinging to every surface

Nelly Bryce

The sweat behind slender necks
My mouth curved into a shape I no longer
understand
Just time for one more
There was always just time for one more

Shoes held to stagger happily home as the sun
came up
A tangled mass of arms
Made-up lines meant only for ourselves
And yet there was no more after that night was
there
The wrong bodies pushing hard against each other
The wrong place at the wrong time

My hand flinches and lands on my stomach
An ice cream van has arrived outside the window
It's playing a tinny tune which I can't quite place
A woman's voice battles heroically
before giving in to the persistent nagging
Sometimes easier that way
I imagine the cone, drizzled in blood-red sauce,
sickly sweet
melting before she has even paid the bill
I used to quite like ice cream
Perhaps I will try again tonight
He'll be eager to go back out and get me some
"Anything to make you happy," he'll chirp

A car door slams and now comes the voice
I drag an arm across my face and tie back my hair
Urgently cram the last items into the only

remaining bin bag
I'll force it into the bottom of the outside bin
Not now, when it's dark
My uneven weight sways to one side as I lever
myself up
Dwell for a second on how strangely natural the
movement felt
for once

Standing, I survey my achievements from the
doorway
The room is now almost clutter-free
When our normal friends come round in the next
few weeks
they'll swoon at our décor choices
and say out loud that they wish they had my good
taste
And he'll look at me with adoring eyes
whilst rocking his perfect baby on his shoulder
Perhaps they'll ask why we chose this room
out of all the others
And I'll reply that it had the best light
And that it wasn't too much to ask, not really
And they'll all laugh and agree and that will be
nice
Or perhaps I won't
because we'll never make it up here
I'll be too busy making everyone a drink.

I don't want to be more than *just a mother.*
I want *just a mother* to be more than it so often is.

Learning Not To Fake It— An Apology To My Body

I'm the Queen of faking it. See how I laugh with my kids about loving my ass as they wobble me with their fingers and I brush them away. Slide the comment about my awful nails to my sister barely seen, yeah I'll have cake too please, how's your week been? Tell my husband how great I look naked - with the lights out. I'll wear tight Lycra to run, yeah my legs look firm and strong but say nothing of the fact I'll pass out before removing this long sleeved top. And no, I don't want to go in the sea, I'm fine sweating here on the beach where I can pull at my beautiful Instagram worthy summer dress to drown out my silent rage at my post breastfeeding boobs and apologising to you for my make-up less face, but have you seen my waist, that isn't too bad at least.

I'm the Queen of faking it and my body it knows. Knows that I don't adore each fold of its skin, the cellulite on my thighs, the thinning of the hair around my forehead, the lines around my eyes. I pinch my stomach where my babies have been and say out loud that I am proud that this was their home, and then what happens next, as I get dressed, it shows.
That ours is a loveless marriage of necessity, a salad when I wanted desert, a coffee when I really

wanted tea, but I'll drink it anyway, to be polite.
Deny the bitterness that coats my tongue and the
chocolate coated criticism which I shake across
every surface, under my breath. That I still crave
the picture on the front of the packet, a longing
which I can't fulfil but have learnt to swallow
down nonetheless.

I am so tired of faking it. Can we start over again,
figure out where and why it went so wrong, and
how to put things right? I want to see photos of
you and my heart to race, I want to take photos
of you, I want to pin you up on my wall and
daydream about your curves during work calls,
I want to text you late at night and beg for you
to come over so that I can devour you, all of you,
strip you down and obsess over the way your
strength feels beneath my teeth. Greedily lap you
up, abandoning all etiquette and eating with my
fingers, shudder beneath the sheets and strike
the sky with full-bodied fireworks. I want to lie
in your arms as the sun comes up and then stroll
comfortably for breakfast hand in hand, teaching
young girls who stop and stare, that no other love
will ever compare, to this.

True Mother Love

the touch of your skin
so soft
in the creases

and the
perfect rolls of body
and the
perfect instinctual tears
and the
perfect utter joy
spread over
constant wonder

abundant love and patience
I have
for you

whisper who you are
and I will listen
whisper what you want
and I will give it
whisper where you hope to go
and I will carry you
wherever it takes

I will choose you
again
and again

for you are all mine
my love

and only then
only this way
can I teach
can I show them that
this
is how they too
can be all theirs.

Family-sized Shop

"How many do you have?" she asks,
our lives separated by a conveyor belt, at least 25
years and the rest.
I wonder if it's the dark circles under my eyes, or
that I haven't lost that distracted edginess which
comes from years of borrowing time?
A pack of cartoon covered yoghurts slide towards
me, containing the answer I want.
"Four," I reply, looking to hold her gaze like a
child who believes they have done well on a test.
I wait for her to pass me back some names or ages
of her own, so that we can share the playing field
and I can fake enthusiasm for something 'funny'
one of them said.
A 2 kg bag of potatoes has become lodged at the
top of the ramp until, with one adept nudge, she
sends them my way.
"I never had any children."
We exist for a single beat before I throw the
potatoes into my bag, crushing everything
underneath, and she continues to scan, the beeps
so steady and clear they wouldn't be out of place
in a hospital ward; shopping skidding across
polished metal into my fumbling hands.
"I bet that, saved you...."
Words stick to the roof of my mouth, but I force
a few out misshapen, unsure if they are even
audible.
I've not brought my Bags for Life, and am now

struggling to cram trays of raw meat in with a
flowered summer dress I grabbed on a whim.
She waits patiently, replaces her pen, surveys her
surroundings, says nothing but,
"Would you like a receipt?"
I mumble thanks, but no, thanks, and manhandle
the last few bags into my trolley.
I leave her with an attempt at my cheeriest
goodbye.
I think about her all the way back to the car.
Imagining all the years she has spent delivering
that line,
sliding it in amongst the baked beans and the
heavily processed white bread,
waiting for the response she deserves.
"I bet that saved you a fortune," I want to add.
"It's not everything, I want to tell her, it's great,
but it's not everything."
I remember nothing of my drive home but later,
surrounded by piles of unfinished work
I slowly begin to do the unpacking, and am so
grateful for the years she has spent teaching
women like me
not to reply at all.

There's a Man at Our Baby Class

He sits down heavily
like a seagull amongst the pigeons.
Strangely large feet on the pretty sparkly rug
laid out for the mornings' session.

The leader makes a fuss of him,
she is being kind, but I can't stop imagining
a group of men in a boardroom
asking the single woman present to take notes.

The other mums too are slightly restless,
intrigued by this outsider who has broken into
their bubble.

I notice that he doesn't sing along to the songs.
Perhaps he doesn't know them yet,
or perhaps the songs he'd sing would be different.

I'm reminded that someone once called the police
to check on my brother
when he was playing hide-and-seek
with his young kids in the park,
then realise too late that I'm staring at the small
plastic drum
he is single-handedly banging to the AHH's of a
few of the others.

He meets my eye and I give him what I hope is
a 'you're welcome here' smile.

The class ends and the leader seems keen to check
he approved of her performance.

No one asks if he'll be back next week.

She believed that She could be a Good Mother:

So she had a baby
And she put on some pregnancy weight
And she breastfed her baby
And she shared immaculate photos
And she rushed straight back to work
And she went to some baby classes
And she worked full time
And she had another baby
And she ran an entire household
And she provided fully for her family
And she gave her whole body to others
And she gave all her time to her children
And she showed her children love
And she visited the places allowed
And she did not often sit down
And she kept it real by hating motherhood
And so she became more exhausted
until one afternoon

She realised all that was left of her goodness on a faded
maternal advice poster on the wall

and reached for all the other hands with the bitten
down fingernails to rip it down

since they did not put it up there after all.

but was careful to ensure she had a baby
but did not carry too much pregnancy weight
but also bottle-fed her baby
but also refused the help she wasn't offered
but also spent enough time at home
but also not to some baby classes
but also stayed at home full time
but not too many more babies
but demanded no help in running a household
but also married and relied on a Good Father
but still kept her own body for herself
but also exercised and practised self-care
but did not show love to herself
but was not seen or heard in the places allowed
but did not say that she did not often sit down
but also kept it real by loving motherhood
each month and each day and each hour
sat in a doctor's waiting room

Words and Deeds

Can we put down their devices
and pick up our chosen tools
Put our feet straight to the floor
and break up all their rules

Can we open our eyes wider
and see that progress it is slipping
note the ones who fight the hardest
keep their energies from dipping

Can we recognise a hopelessness
and find instead an action
Can we stop accepting compromise
come together without fraction

Can we mess with all their systems
and none of us spend a penny
Can we acknowledge individual pain
and also healing for the many

Can we celebrate our achievements
and be allowed to get it wrong
Can we fight the shame and guilt
that stop us from feeling strong

Can we lean into our anger
and let it spill right out
Use our work, our homes, our voices
Can we write and stamp and shout

Can we remember we are plenty
so when we think we don't know how
Can we grab each other's hands
Demand the change that we want now

Role: Male Ally

This is not a new position, but one which we are re-advertising due to a smaller than hoped response to previous adverts.

Job requirements:

- To educate yourself on how you are complicit within the system of gender inequality.
- To understand how privilege may have resulted in your being blind to the problem, to empathise with the women who are fighting it every single day.
- To use your voice and privilege to speak up and advocate for women, amongst other duties. Note— it is not enough to simply not partake in sexism personally, which is an important, but more junior role.
- To actively stand alongside women in the fight for gender equality.

Terms: Permanent and flexible. Goes without saying. Where have you been?

Location: Gender inequality starts at home. Must be willing to review behaviour in all areas of life, including the home and workplace.

Rewards and benefits: A kinder, more caring planet on which we can ALL live. Actually, just having a planet full stop. If you are looking for brand exposure or any sort of capitalist gains because feminism is "having a moment" you need not apply.

Also, this is not about you.

Past experience: None necessary. You definitely need not have a daughter, sister, girlfriend, or wife to apply. Just be a decent human being.

Closing date: There isn't one, but candidates willing to start with immediate effect would be preferred. This is a crucial role, and we've been waiting too long already.

Set Up to Compete

I'm competing with you every time that we meet.
Wondering if my size, my hair, the clothes I wear
can be better, can mean I am more worthy, more
complete.
I'm competing with you in a race that doesn't
exist, a phantom event where I'm the only runner
on the starting line.
Or perhaps there are others, perhaps we are all
competing, just in parallel races at a different
time.
I'm competing with you in spite of myself.
Because there's only so much room upon the shelf.
Limited seats at the table, I've been told, places at
the top.
We can't all survive, so some must drop.
But I'm a reluctant competitor, an awkward pawn.
In a game that I didn't really sign up for at all.
In the arena we're manipulated, set up to fight.
To bring each other down so only one group's
alright.
My competing with you fills me with shame, I
know it's wrong, so don't speak, and then they
keep us down again.
But these competitors are fierce, these
competitors are strong, and it's the opposite side
that wants to fear they don't belong.
I will no longer compete with you my sisters,

won't bring you down, so I can rise.
It's together that we all win, when we break these
competition lies.

The Becoming of a Poster Girl

All the boys I knew then had posters of girls
bronzed and tight
wearing hot pants and tiny tops that might've fit
my Barbies
sat with dust gathering on their miles of limbs

These girls

Leaning over in ways that I had never felt - tying
my laces or kicking a ball
they'd be touching their own bodies like they
weren't their own bodies
stood with their hands in their own hair
I saw what I thought was power
and would simmer in my own desire
to cut it out

I'd stare for hours with scissors poised in my head
as I lounged on my first boyfriend's blue
chequered bed
snipping my way up smooth thighs
            around the soft skin of a peachy bum
and impossibly round breasts
            up and over the thick Rapunzel-like
hair
careful not to nick
            this perfect outline of a girl

so unbearably slick I'd get at
cutting

During classes at school
in the park with my mates
in Topshop on a Saturday afternoon
all of us were, I think
always staring, always sculpting

So much time I'd spend
I'd lie awake at night
cutting
dream of neatly shaping
cutting
my own edges

I knew these Poster Girls were not meant for me
but top shelves didn't stop them from starting to
be
I'd freeze-frame the ads on TV
would cut out the ways the boys talked about the
girls in their magazines
from my own magazines
stick their words into my own diary
place them under the plate from which I'd eat my
tea to encourage me not to
wear my contempt for their contoured arms under
a cardigan
that would remind me to feel the cold even when I
was not

These Poster Girls

I would cut them out whole

larger than myself
these picture-perfect Poster Girls
now up on my own walls

Cut   cut   cut

Myself into pieces

Scattered body parts

Face down

across the floor

limbs disjointed

the natural curve of
a stomach lost

squares of bare skin now trapped under the door

pieces stuck to the bottom of feet and trampled

around the house

segments of discarded thigh

crumpled and swept purposefully beneath clothes

I left my self lying on my bedroom floor.

So that years later
armed with the strongest glue
with my own children standing beneath me
gazing up at empty walls
it has taken what has felt like forever
to even start to stick back together

the perfect Poster Girl.

Every Day We Die A Little

every day we die a little / I push metal grips into
my hair, so the greys can be denied / like the strain
across my back as I reach down for a dropped
sock / attempt to cement over riverbeds of smiles
where my eyes once thought I was growing more
and more alive with every day that passed / not
realising that the water never flows back / but
that every day we die a little / and yet somehow
there I was / and here I am / waiting / for the
kettle to boil / for the reply to the letter which
I did not write to fail to arrive in the post / for
the piano I never learnt to play / to play / to play
a breathtaking piece to accompany the dreams
kept firmly inside the locked book beside my bed
/ saved for a rainy day / or a sunny day / a day with
a little less on / a pay day / a hundred pay days / a
day when the moon is perfectly visible at night / a
day with cake and candles / a day without / a day
that someone else decides is right / a day when
this list is complete / a graduation day / another
day / another day / another day to die a little / like
I have been since the very first / and did I not used
to know this / the way I'd tackle the climbing of a
tree / or pause to feed sugar water from a spoon to
a fallen honey bee / believe that I could fit my tiny
nail into the stem of a daisy / thread stem upon
stem the chain growing with my delight / and then
hang such delicate truths around my wrist / so that
sometimes they'd break, and I could start again /

dancing them into life / racing with them through
decades of grass stained knees / so at ease with the
fact that every day we die a little / that every day
we can live a little / bit more.

Real Men

don't laugh at that joke about the girl on
reception.
Change a nappy using one they picked up from the
shop
after finishing the pack the night before.
Need a tissue for the end of The Lion King.
Ask why there aren't any women in the meeting,
but don't ask any women to thank them for asking.
Know that Tuesday is book swap day and that,
on a Thursday morning, the youngest waves at the
bin truck.
Enjoy snuggling under their blanket on the sofa
after they've helped to clean up the plates,
on which the world was handed to them.

Worship

See this woman who can temper storms
and catch fallen stars.
Who carries more than a single life's work
upon her back.
Who will at times grow a whole universe
beneath her skin.
Navigate a lifetime of love without a map.
Why do we not admire the entirety of her form?
As she sways and swoops?
As with the beauty of nature that we spend
so long capturing.
Upholding as truth that the world is good.
As if she is not the reason
that we have the world at all.

When all is said and done
I wish for you this:

A long pause.
A tell me more.
A vow to attend.
An abandoned script.
A first word.
A last word.
A steady silence
for you to be heard.

About the Author

Nelly Bryce is a writer, a poet, a mother of four living in Manchester, UK. In 2016, after spending most of her career working in HR (learning and development), she left her corporate job to launch Guilty Mothers Club, a community for modern feminist mothers. Nelly is a journaling addict, who is never far from a notebook and pen. She enjoys encouraging other women to write themselves better stories and get shit down on the page. This is her first book of poetry.

Printed in Poland
by Amazon Fulfillment
Poland Sp. z o.o., Wrocław

89964389R00115